EUROPE

EUROPE

THE SHATTERING OF ILLUSIONS

VÁCLAV KLAUS
President of the Czech Republic

Translated by Ondřej Hejma

B L O O M S B U R Y
LONDON · NEW DELHI · NEW YORK · SYDNEY

© Václav Klaus, 2011

This English translation © Bloomsbury Publishing Plc, 2012

First published as *Evropská integrace bez iluzí* in 2011 by
Euromedia Group k.s., Nádražní 32, CZ-150 00 Praha 5,
Czech Republic

This edition first published in Great Britain 2012

The moral right of the author has been asserted

A Continuum book

Bloomsbury Publishing Plc
50 Bedford Square
London WC1B 3DP

www.bloomsbury.com

Bloomsbury Publishing, London, New Delhi, New York and Sydney

A CIP record for this book is available from the British Library.

ISBN 978 1 4081 8764 7

10 9 8 7 6 5 4 3 2 1

Typeset by Fakenham Prepress Solutions, Fakenham, Norfolk
NR21 8NN
Printed and bound by CPI Group (UK) Ltd, Croydon, CR0 4YY

Translation by Ondřej Hejma

The author is grateful to Lord Monckton for editorial assistance with
this book.

Contents

Foreword by Christopher Booker

As the European Union faces by far the most serious crisis in its history, this book could not be more timely. There could be few better ways to introduce its author, Václav Klaus, to an English-speaking audience than to recall a bizarre episode in December 2008 which conveys just why the President of the Czech Republic has come to occupy a unique position among the world's senior politicians.

Just before Christmas that year the leaders of the main political groupings in the European Parliament, led by the Parliament's president, Hans-Gert Pöttering, flew to Prague to meet President Klaus at his imposing palace looking down over the Czech capital.

The purpose of their mission was to discuss with him what would happen when, the following month, the Czech government was due to take over the rotating presidency of the EU's Council of Ministers, responsible for deciding the EU's list of priorities over the next six months.

Two issues in particular were top of the EU agenda at that time. One was that 'Constitution for Europe' which, after years of tortuous negotiation, had twice been rejected in referendums by the voters of France and the Netherlands. But now that it had been resurrected as the 'Lisbon Treaty', the Czech parliament was the only one left in Europe which had not ratified it – although it had again recently been rejected in a referendum by the voters of Ireland. Nothing was more important to the EU's ruling elite than that the ratification process should now be completed as quickly as possible.

The other pressing issue was the hugely important package of radical measures agreed in principle by the EU's leaders the previous year as their response to the threat of global warming. Would the Czech government do all in its power to ensure that these were soon turned into EU law?

On each of these issues, President Klaus was very much the EU's odd man out. As an academic economist, he had lived much of his life under a Communist dictatorship. After his country's liberation from totalitarian rule in 1989, he had become its prime minister between 1992 and 1997 – responsible for his country's application to join the EU – before succeeding the playwright Václav Havel in 2003 as its second president and head of state.

But after the Czechs joined the EU in 2004, Klaus had come to be viewed by his European colleagues with a mixture of puzzlement, suspicion and even downright hostility. This was, firstly because, alone among the EU's leaders, he was an avowed 'Euro-sceptic'. He had frequently warned that the full political union the EU was moving towards was becoming much too reminiscent of the Communist system he knew so well. It was bent on replacing Europe's nation states with a highly bureaucratic, centralised form of supra-national government, run by a political class which appeared to have little concern for the wishes of the peoples it ruled over.

The other issue which isolated Klaus from his colleagues was the EU's proclaimed desire to 'lead the world in the fight against climate change'. As he had set out in a recent book, *Blue Planet in Green Shackles,* this also reminded him uncomfortably of Communism, as a rigid ideology which was being used to justify ever more regulation and state control, threatening Europe's freedom, democracy and economic prosperity.

The MEPs arrived to meet the Czech president in Hradcany Castle, which stands high above the beautiful city of Prague, part of the complex of majestic buildings which for centuries had symbolised Czech national identity. The only flag permitted to fly over Klaus's presidential palace was that of the Czech Republic. There was no place for the 'ring of stars' of the European Union, although in the city below this hung outside every government ministry alongside the Czech flag, to symbolise the extent to which the country's government was now shared with that centred in Brussels.

Among the senior MEPs who came to Hradcany that day was the leader of the Green grouping in the European Parliament. Daniel Cohn-Bendit, born in Germany but now living in France, had first come to prominence as a student agitator on the Paris barricades in 1968. On the plane on the way to Prague, he had spoken loudly within the earshot of journalists about how he was planning a dramatic gesture to symbolise just what he and his colleagues thought about President Klaus.

When they entered the grand room looking out over the city where the meeting was to take place, they were greeted by Klaus with his customary genial courtesy. He assured them that, when the Czech Republic assumed the EU Presidency, 'I am convinced that we will succeed in holding the Presidency without any problems'. The Czech government and all the state institutions were 'preparing themselves responsibly' for the role they were about to play.

Cohn-Bendit then staged his planned ambush. He brusquely plonked down in front of Klaus an EU flag, sarcastically observing how much in evidence it seemed to be around his palace. It was a studied insult, not too dissimilar to a Franco-German MEP being invited to meet the Queen at Buckingham Palace and presenting her with a 'ring of stars' flag, insisting that she hoist it over the palace alongside the Royal Standard.

Cohn-Bendit warned Klaus that the Czechs would be expected to put through the EU's 'climate change package' without interference. 'You can believe what you want', he scornfully told the president, 'but I don't believe, I know that global warming is a reality'. 'My view', he went on, 'is based on scientific views and the majority approval of the EU Parliament'.

Cohn-Bendit then moved on to the Lisbon Treaty. 'I don't care about your opinions on it', he said. What he wanted to know was, if the Czech Parliament approves the treaty in February, 'will you respect the will of the representatives of the people?' He continued by reprimanding the president for recently meeting in Ireland with Declan Ganley, the millionaire leader of the 'No' campaign in the referendum which had just resulted in Irish rejection of the Lisbon Treaty. It had been quite improper, Cohn-Bendit told the president, for him to have met with someone whose 'finances come from problematic sources'.

Visibly taken aback by this onslaught, Klaus observed 'I must say that no one has talked to me in such a style and tone in the past six years.

You are not on the barricades in Paris here. I thought that such manners ended for us 19 years ago' (when Communism fell).

When Klaus suggested to the leader of the MEPs, that perhaps it was time for someone else to take the floor, Pöttering replied 'anyone from the members of the Parliament can ask you what he likes', and invited Cohn-Bendit to continue. 'This is incredible', said Klaus, 'I have never experienced anything like this before'.

After a further exchange, in which Cohn-Bendit compared Klaus unfavourably with his predecessor, President Havel, he gave way to an Irish MEP, Brian Crowley, who began by saying 'all his life my father fought against the British domination (of Ireland). That is why I dare to say that the Irish wish for the Lisbon Treaty. It was an insult, Mr President, to me and the Irish people what you said during your state visit to Ireland'. Klaus repeated that he had not experienced anything like this for 19 years and that it seemed we were no longer living in a democracy, but that it was 'post-democracy which rules the EU'.

On the EU constitution, Klaus recalled that three countries had voted against it, and that if Mr Crowley wanted to talk about insults to the Irish people, 'the biggest insult to the Irish people is not to accept the result of the Irish referendum'. This provoked from Crowley the angry retort 'you will not tell me what the Irish think. As an Irishman, I know it best'.

Shortly afterwards Pöttering closed the meeting by saying that, although he wanted to leave the room 'in good terms', it was quite unacceptable to compare himself and his colleagues with the Soviet Union. Klaus replied that he had not mentioned the Soviet Union: 'I only said that I had not experienced such an atmosphere, such a style of debate, in the Czech Republic in the last 19 years'.

*****

It is not inappropriate to give such a detailed description of this remarkable episode because it so vividly illustrates just what a curious position President Klaus has recently come to occupy in the politics of contemporary Europe.

As it happens, I know the splendid room in which that confrontation took place, because I myself first met him there after he had arranged for a Czech translation of *The Great Deception*, a history of 'the European project' I had written with Richard North.

To launch the book, we drove that afternoon down into Prague's Old Town where, in a large hall, Klaus once a month held an open seminar for anyone wishing to take part. There was no very obvious security presence, as there would have been when the head of state of almost any other country appeared in public. Some 400 people filled the hall. There were a few speeches (mine was the only one in English), and what particularly struck me, as Klaus himself spoke and answered questions from the audience, was how often his remarks met with an amused ripple of laughter.

I could not imagine any other head of state or leading politician in Europe making himself regularly available like this to anyone choosing to walk in off the street – or for that matter being regarded with such obvious warmth and appreciation.

The next time I saw President Klaus was three years later in New York, where he addressed a conference of 'climate sceptics' organised by the Heartland Institute. The other speakers included a good many eminent scientists from all over the world who explained why they could not agree with the accepted scientific orthodoxy on global warming. But what only President Klaus was able to tell the 800 people in the audience was that a week earlier he had been with all the world's political leaders at that year's meeting of the World Economic Forum in Davos.

He recalled how, as he mingled with President Obama and other world leaders, he had tried to engage them on the questionable scientific credentials of the case for man-made global warming, about which he was very well informed, and the very serious political and economic implications to which they were giving rise (this was just months before the Copenhagen climate conference which was to collapse in disarray the following December). But not one of the leaders he spoke to seemed prepared to discuss such matters.

Klaus thus stands out as a politician who has

long been highly critical of what have been two of the most powerful and influential belief-systems of our time. But each of them in recent years has come under more profound questioning than ever before. Not only has the scientific case for man-made global warming been called increasingly into question, as the predictions of the computer models on which it rests are not borne out by the observed data. Since the failure to agree a treaty at Copenhagen in 2009, attempts to concert any global response to climate change have all but fallen apart. This has left the European Union virtually alone in its readiness to continue imposing the most drastic restrictions on its economic activity, to meet a problem which it now seems may have been imaginary.

Similarly, the drive to weld the nations of Europe together in 'ever closer union' has landed the 'European project' in by far the most intractable crisis it has faced in all the 50 years since it had been launched on its way: one it has brought on itself through the most reckless of all the steps it has taken to further full political and economic integration, the creation of a single currency.

In this book President Klaus sets out his thoughts on why he sees the 'European project' as having been based on a fundamental misconception, one which has in many ways produced a strange echo of that rigidly bureaucratic, illiberal, anti-democratic and dehumanised system of government which eventually brought about its own downfall with the collapse of Communism. For 'Europe' to survive, he argues, it would need to reform itself completely, into an intergovernmental confederation of democratic nation states.

This was, of course, precisely the kind of Europe which Jean Monnet was determined to eliminate when, back in the 1950s, he launched on its way that supra-national form of government we have seen gradually taking shape ever since – and which has now come to such a fateful impasse.

What was really significant about that confrontation in 2008 between President Klaus and those MEPs was the way it revealed the Euro-elite's inability to accept that anyone can be allowed to hold different views from their own – on the Lisbon treaty, global warming or anything else. As we in Britain have come to see, from the way our own political parties are run, when it comes to 'Europe' the system simply cannot tolerate any kind of opposition. Everything must be decided by 'consensus', directed from the top. There can only be one approved 'party line'. Apart from a few little powerless dissidents round the edges, the EU is thus in essence a one-party state.

The glory of Václav Klaus is that he recognises this, and what extraordinary dangers it poses for all our futures. He is the one senior European politician who, from within the system, has nevertheless been able to continue speaking out for those all-important values and concepts to which his colleagues have become virtually oblivious – such as liberty, democracy and the wishes of the people they claim to represent.

Yet on these two great issues of our time, history is beginning to show that Klaus was the one who got it right. That is why, at this grave juncture in European history, the thoughts of the man who has for so long been pointing out that the emperor has no clothes are very much worthy of our attention.

INTRODUCTION

Why this philippic now?

European history is moving extremely fast right now. No week passes without some disappointing – if not actually catastrophic – news. As I write these lines, all the internet news services are reporting the collapse of the Belgian bank Dexia, whose chief, Jean-Luc Dehaene, is a well-known eurocrat and former prime minister of Belgium, with whom I have repeatedly clashed over various European issues. He would have done better if he had stayed in politics, I guess.

Until recently, no week passed without a meeting of President Sarkozy and Chancellor Merkel who 'solve' the future of our continent for us and without us with worried faces and well-practiced smiles full of promises. No week passes without a surprising electoral victory for some new populist group. In radio news, I have just heard a report on the Polish parliamentary elections. A new party, launching its first initiative, wants to remove the Christian Cross from the Parliament building. No week – indeed no day – passes without the leaders of the European Union releasing some very dubious statement, trying to calm the public by claiming that officials have everything under control.

Despite these assurances from European politicians, the current economic stagnation and the general dismay of the people are real. Permanent and deep disputes both within and among the continent's countries are real as well, when it comes to the question of where to go next and how to get there. Another striking element of today's reality is the growing public dissatisfaction over the progress of European integration. Many now see a united Europe as a blind alley. Public criticism, however, wrongly concentrates on integration's most visibly dysfunctional project, the euro. There are other huge problems, such as the Schengen area, but the current European crisis is much broader than these two projects.

Apart from the powerful coalition of political and financial vested interests, that depend on the EU for their existence – consisting of EU politicians and bureaucrats as well as media, businesses, artistic, scientific, environmental and other groups living on parasitic terms off the various European projects – hardly anybody defends the current developments in Europe. The only exception are perhaps those who dream of a united mankind and who, together with Karl Marx, have been dreaming for 150 years about the moment when the State finally withers away. In contrast to Marx, however, they do not believe that salvation will come from the proletariat: they humbly suggest it will come from themselves.

The criticism of the European Union we hear these days is too cautious, mostly focusing on outward, superficial and partial issues. The essence of the problem remains taboo. The sacred mantra of the eurocrats has survived intact for more than half a century: European integration is the Good, regardless of what it brings, whether things go well or not, whether there are many critics or few, whether the European Union is detached and alienated from its people more and more, whether the cost of maintaining individual integration projects is too high, whether the promised effects of European integration differ from reality in any way.

The euro is an especially charming example. Everybody has forgotten the authoritarian warnings the eurocrats were giving us, the sceptics, ten years ago. They told us that those who would not use the euro would pay for it dearly! It is more than obvious today, that none of the European countries that have kept their own currency is going through a credit crisis comparable to Greece, Italy, Spain, Portugal, Ireland … Latvia did undergo a similar crisis even before the global financial and monetary crisis. It did not use the euro, but its exchange rate was fixed to the euro, which is almost the same thing.

This failure to focus on the defects in the European project has to stop, even though the solution will be long and difficult. It must be a long-term process, because we are not talking about ideal solutions, feasible in a vacuum or on a chessboard. We are talking about real solutions for real people. Such solutions cannot have theoretical beauty and purity, but their direction must be clear-cut and well-defined and in that sense beautiful.

Right now there is one proposed solution, enforced by the European establishment, never mind the rhetoric differences: transition from a monetary union to a fiscal union based on transfers and redistribution of wealth. This institutional shift would be anchored in the respective European treaties.

The entire text that follows is a sometimes explicit, sometimes implicit polemic that challenges this attempt to further deepen the process of European integration, which would in all substantial respects finally nullify the importance of nation states by elevating the EU until it became the supreme governing entity in our lives.

This is not a time for half-heartedness or half-measures. More or less courageous critiques of these 'solutions' proposed by the eurocracy will not do. They must be resolutely rejected.

From my position (perhaps lacking enough European solidarity in the eyes of some), I cannot rule out a non-standard, one-time solution for Greece and perhaps other countries, even at the cost of violating all those treaties from Maastricht to Lisbon, which are in the final analysis nothing but a fallible 'human' construction. This 'unclean' solution is acceptable for me as the price for not creating the 'Union of European Post-Democratic Republics'. I might be tempted to call it the UEPDR.

The only lasting and successful solution for the European problem lies in preserving the dominance of states (nation states in most cases), the states of the Portuguese, the Finns, the Spanish, the Irish and other nations and I certainly do not demand that these states should be ethnically homogeneous. All things continental, communitarizing and 'globalizing' must be secondary and derivative. I must point back to my proposal tabled in 2005, during the officially ordained period of 'reflection' on European integration after the voters of France and the Netherlands had rejected the European 'Constitution' in a referendum.

I have offered to create the OES, the Organization of European States.[1] I said then: 'The purpose of membership in the OES must not be the ambition to enforce any form of ideology. It must be built on a common

1. 'Let Us Create a New European Union', Lidové Noviny, 16 June 2005.

faith that member states are capable of acting together in certain areas'.

In the case of Greece, the solution would first have to be in the form of one-time aid, and then, after the most acute stage of the crisis is over, a sovereign Greek decision to leave the eurozone peacefully (or a decision radically to change its domestic policies).

Do not let me be misunderstood. As I shall explain in the following pages I do not fight the European Union or Mr. Van Rompuy or Señor Barroso, I oppose the unfortunate course of events in the evolution of Europe, where the problems are self-evident today. The fate of the Czech nation depends to a large extent on Europe's self-reflection. I do not believe we are determined – by fate or geographic position – to be mere pawns on the European chessboard, somewhere between Moscow and Brussels. The very opposite is true.

I am convinced we have the right and the obligation to look after our interests, given our own unique experience. This requires some courage. There are historical examples to follow. In the complex situation at the turn of the seventies and eighties, Ronald Reagan also refused to bow to the intellectual trends of his time. Let us do the same. I am just reading a recently published book by Joseph Roth, *Die Filiale der Hoelle auf Erden.* He, too, had a feeling that Europe was surrendering. 'It surrenders out of weakness, out of laziness, out of indifference and thoughtlessness'.[2]

This is why I have written this book.

October 2011

---

2. Roth, Joseph (2011), *Die Filiale der Hoelle auf Erden*, Prague: Academia, p. 38.

ONE

How we got here

The past, including the relatively recent past, is being forgotten very quickly. But I am not a historian. That is why I will not focus on details and write 'under the microscope', because a lot of what happened is already irrelevant. I will not seek a detailed breakdown of minute changes and movements in the history of the half-century-long process of European integration. I will not provide an analysis of individual European summits and the treaties that were named after the cities where they took place, because that could drown out the main points. Instead, I will use broader strokes of the brush, trying to outline fundamental changes in trends and tendencies. Others might paint a different picture of the evolution of European integration, but this one is mine. I am convinced it is honest and accurate.

Looking back, we have to realize that in principle the current European integration process, as it was formed after World War II, was nothing new even then. From the point of view of objectives and methods used, it is nothing but a continuation of a long line of persistent and recurring attempts to unite the continent that began with the fall of the universal Roman

Empire. Despite the Empire's fall, its example inspired many a dream of European unification in the years to come. Unlike visions shared by the Habsburgs, Napoleon, Hitler or Stalin, we are now facing the first attempt to unify our continent through peaceful means, by way of agreement among the key power-players. That makes it look deceivingly innocent.

The idea of this post-war European integration has its roots in the 1930s, in the tragic experience of World War I and the Great Depression. This is when we started seeing a growing consensus in some influential French and gradually also British political circles, claiming that the traditional rivalry of European superpowers is destructive and therefore has to be replaced by mutually beneficial agreements based on the status quo and without any outside interference by non-European players, such as the United States or the rising eastern communist power, the Soviet Union.

The emancipation of the defeated Germany, another key European player, was necessary to give life to the new structure. From this point of view, the Peace Treaty of Versailles, the basis for European politics after World War I, looked like a mistake, preventing Germany from taking part in the game. This is also where we find the logic of the policy of appeasement towards Nazi Germany, widely denounced and condemned later. Integrationist aspirations fell by the wayside at the time, mainly because western politicians did not find a partner for their project in Germany. Hitler also wanted a 'new Europe', a Europe completely subordinated to the Third Reich. But he did not care for agreements with others and did not plan to stick to any of them.

After the defeat of Nazism, in a situation completely changed by the Cold War, the pre-war vision of European cooperation was ready for implementation. The defeated, divided, democratic and economically prosperous West Germany, traumatized and paralyzed by its war guilt, became a suitable partner for ideas conceived by the French fathers of European integration, Schuman and Monnet, who had advocated Franco-German cooperation even before and during World War II.

This was a suitable time, when Hitler's imperialistic and totally undemocratic ambition to create

15

a 'new Europe' – leading to the horrible war that almost ruined the continent – was dramatically and emphatically defeated. This was a time when many in Europe still remembered the less than wonderful years before Hitler, too. The Great Depression, protectionism, mercantilistic isolation, voluntary devaluations in the hope of one-sided advantage (however temporary), all that had given rise to political chaos, terrifying unemployment and economic downturn. The feeling of total hopelessness opened the door to despotic, undemocratic – and no less imperialistic – Communism, whose contagion was close to spreading from eastern and central Europe to the western part of the continent after the war.

Westerners thought of Europe as being Western Europe only. They did not consider the territories beyond the Rhine and the Elbe and north of the Danube to be very European. Here I cannot resist quoting Konrad Adenauer, who once spoke of 'the Asian steppes on the eastern bank of the Elbe'. In parallel with the first attempts at post-war integration in Western Europe, the new Soviet empire was expanding too, including voluntary or involuntary satellites such as our country, Czechoslovakia. This threat from the East pulled Western Europe together, providing the motivation for various forms of joint action.

The basis for the European integration project consisted of several very doubtful ideas, whose negative effects are very clear today.

The authors of the concept of European integration managed to short-circuit the minds of the people, making a link between Hitler's aggressive nationalism (nationalism of the totally negative type) and the traditional nation state, calling into question the existence of nation states in general.

Of the many fatal mistakes and lies that have always underpinned the evolution of the European Union, this was one of the worst. It led to total obliteration of the enormous positive energy of national sentiments, or positive nationalism, (where the state is based on national identity and loyalty), ignoring the fact that throughout human history this form of statehood is the much more common standard.[1] (John Fonte provides useful inspiration when he writes about the difference between positive and negative nationalism as well as national identity in his recent book.[2])

At that time, the founders of the idea of European integration had an outlook – perhaps sincere to a degree – that saw only negatives in the concept of a nation state, and it is no different today. Subsequently they made this view the linchpin of the entire concept, further supported by the idea that European states are small and unable to compete with superpowers

1. I have been troubled for a long time by the relatively neutral use of the word nationalism in a number of countries (and languages) and the fact that in the Czech context this very word has a clearly negative connotation. I do not use the phrase 'long time' by accident. In the spring of 1969, during my stay at the Cornell University in the United States, I was frequently asked to talk about the 'Prague Spring' of 1968. My description of our ambitions was sometimes seen as an expression of nationalism, a notion I resisted, given my linguistic background, but apparently those who used it on the American side did not see any harm in it.
2. See Fonte, John (2011), *Sovereignty or Submission*, New York: Encounter Books, Chapter 3.

like the United States or the Soviet Union (the BRIC countries, China, India, Russia and Brazil were not considered as competitors then).

That is why – truly in the spirit of Orwell's genius in his literary concept of *1984* – the argument that only a united Europe would be big enough and strong enough to compete with these big countries was attractive to some. I do not know in what way and at what level countries like Denmark, Austria, Lithuania or the Czech Republic should compete with the superpowers. People living in these countries never had any such ambition then or now. Some politicians, though, may have had such aspirations then, and the European establishment certainly has them now.

It was especially for this reason that the initial idea of mere economic integration, i.e. economic cooperation, mutual opening up, liberalization of trade, and elimination of barriers to the free flow of goods and services, enjoyed such massive support at the beginning. It was understood that this step was economically desirable. It was also thought that countries linked together economically (and

19

therefore depending on each other to a certain degree) would most certainly never wage war on one another.

I am often surprised when my critique of how Europe works is countered by arguments that I may be right, but at least we have peace. I do not have to tell you how often we heard similar arguments under Communism, and how difficult it was to swallow that fallacy.

It was on the basis of this idea of economic integration in the cause of peace that the first form of European integration, built on the inter-governmental principle, was born in 1957, and called the European Economic Community (EEC). Here I am leaving aside earlier attempts at integration such as the European Coal and Steel Community (ECSC) and the parallel structure of the European Atomic Energy Community (EURATOM).

At that time, the letter E for 'Economic' in the organization's name was the fundamental defining element and was considered quite sufficient, too. I know the argument – and there is ample evidence of it in earlier statements by the 'founding fathers' – that there were politicians even at that time who saw this phase of integration as a tactical interim stage, a phase that could not be skipped either because the politicians and citizens of individual countries did not wish for further integration at the time, or because it is generally necessary to proceed from simpler forms to more complex structures.

It is for that reason that higher forms of integration were not feasible then, even if some desired them. One of the 'founding fathers', Jean Monnet, said these famous words on 30 April 1952, at the UN: 'Europe's nations should be led towards a superstate, without their people understanding what is happening'. Monnet's 'sincere' words should not be forgotten.

Nevertheless, I think the EEC (minus the countries of central and eastern Europe who, led by the Soviet Union, formed Comecon roughly at the same time) was in line with the reality of the time and enjoyed authentic popular support in the original six countries. Closer economic integration was rational and

21

therefore beneficial. The core concepts of economic integration were the free-trade area, and the common agricultural policy (a policy based on planning, control and subsidies, not dissimilar to what we knew under Communism). I repeat that I am only describing the outlines of the system, this is not a detailed list of the shared activities orchestrated and performed by Brussels.

It is also widely known that not everybody was in favor of this kind of economic integration at the time. As soon as the EEC started displaying some of its more ambitious features, a parallel alternative was born in 1960, known as EFTA, the European Free Trade Association, which – led by England – made it clear from the start that integration should remain limited to economic matters only. When England reconsidered its position, under the reign of the conservative premier Edward Heath at the beginning of the 1970s, and 'changed clubs' in favor of the EEC, all chances for an alternative project of European integration were doomed, even though EFTA – consisting of Switzerland, Iceland, Norway and Liechtenstein – has survived until today. I remember well being lured as Czech premier by these countries – especially by the Swiss – to join EFTA at the beginning of the 1990s.

By the logic of things, the EEC – although still a 'mild' form of integration – started building its empires and offices, creating its own bureaucracy, its 'European' politicians, its lobbyists, its embedded media dependent on the European institutions. In other words it became an enterprise by and for itself (and a major employer).

These people, as well the institutions they worked for, started living their own lives. Slowly and cautiously at first, but ever so rapidly and consistently later, they were gaining new independence, shedding the original mantle of mere servants to the member states. At the same time we saw the implicit, gradual and largely invisible birth of the ideology which I call europeism[3] with new horizons in time and space, drafting and promoting the contours of

3. See my text 'What is europeism?', Mladá Fronta Dnes, available at www.klaus.cz [8 April 2006], and in the book *Year Four*, (2007), Prague: Euromedia.

23

future integration. An important moment can be seen in the so-called Werner report, dated 1970, where – among other things – the idea of a common European currency appears for the first time.[4]

The second phase in the development of European integration was the elimination of the letter E for 'Economic' from its title. This transformation of the EEC to EC, the European Community (unifying all three of its predecessors) was unquestionably intended to show that European integration would not in future confine itself to economic matters only. This transformation took place in the late 1960s and early 1970s.

At about the same time, the original six founding countries were joined by Great Britain, Ireland and Denmark (on 1 January 1973). The number

4. I met Pierre Werner, an 85-year old gentleman, in 1998 at a conference in Luxembourg and he uttered a remarkable sentence then: the essence of the whole European problem is to end the eternal conflict between the German and the Roman world. He did concede this was not such a burning issue for the Slavs or the English.

of member countries was stabilized at nine for almost a decade. Nothing changed in the quality of the EC when three more countries joined – Greece in 1981 and, in 1986, Spain and Portugal. The biggest change was perhaps the growing intra-European redistribution of wealth, a form of direct, cash aid to the three under-developed southern countries. Until today's bailout of Greece, no comparable aid to poorer countries was seen thereafter – a disappointment for the countries of central and eastern Europe who had expected the same generosity when they joined the EU 20 years later.

The letter C still remained part of the name of this integrating group, indicating it was still a 'community' of countries, not an entity robbing individual states of their sovereignty, not a federation, not a superstate. A citizen still remained a citizen of his or her country, regions remained regions (provinces, or Bundeslaender) of their states. This was still a Europe of states, not a Europe of regions, much less a Europe of individual citizens.

The bureaucracy in Brussels gained muscle (especially after the ratification in February

1986 of the 'Single European Act', which became the basis for the 'single European market'). Its power grew rapidly with the number of people working and making their living in or from Brussels. The influence of europeism – not the same thing as being European – was growing as well, and all this peaked in the activities of Jacques Delors, the principal ideologue and director of this radical leap forward. The leap was eventually taken in the form of the so-called Maastricht Treaty of 1991.

The European Community (EC) became the European Union (EU). Most Europeans did not perhaps even notice it. For a start, we were very preoccupied with the radical and difficult trans-formation from Communism to a free society and parliamentary democracy. Despite that, it gives me some satisfaction to say that even at the time I made many speeches drawing attention to the difference between intergovernmentalism and supranationalism. I knew Jacques Delors was leading us from the former to the latter.

It was hard to bear – knowing that we would join the EU sooner or later – when Jacques

Delors started looking for the 'soul' of Europe some time around 1992. He knew very well, that firing Europeans up for the idea of the European Union, (as distinct from Europe, which is a natural focus of respect and affection for anyone living there), was impossible with the help of 'base' arguments such as mere economic advantage. Something spiritual was needed, and that is where Delors' 'deification' of Europe comes from.

I know full well that our local opponents of the market and free trade, who had labelled the very system as 'petty grocery', loved this search for the soul of Europe. This group included not only the traditional communist and socialist left but also the new left around President Havel. (I describe this ideology in my book *Where Tomorrow Begins*.[5] I call it havelism.)

More and more people in Europe began to realize, albeit belatedly, that a union is qualitatively different from a mere community of states. The Union clearly began to dominate the individual states, not only by way of changing

5. (2009) Prague: Euromedia.

existing treaties, but also by introducing new legislation, drafting various 'mandatory' documents and thousands of campaigns – be it the promotion of the slogan 'Europe of the regions' (as opposed to states) or the writing of textbooks on European history, in which the existence of individual nations and states is suppressed at will. According to one of those I see on my table, Leonardo da Vinci is a European painter, not an Italian painter. The bureaucracy in Brussels published a map of Europe filled with names of regions instead of states, causing a scandal in the British parliament over the fact that this map mentions England, Wales and Scotland but not Great Britain. The European became primary, the national became secondary. Before Maastricht it had been the other way around.

These are not new thoughts on my part. Ten years ago, in December 2001, I wrote a newspaper article called 'Ten Years After Maastricht', which included this passage:

The ratification of the Maastricht Treaty transformed the European Community into the European Union. Seemingly, only one letter was replaced: the acronym changed from EC to EU.

This happened at the very end of the ill-fated 20th century, during which Europe almost ruined itself twice. It happened at a time when Communism was finished once and for all, when it seemed freedom prevailed for good, when we hoped that dangerous ideologies of the past were finally discredited. Unfortunately this was not the case ... The spirit of the time (and here the German word *Zeitgeist* fits rather well) has shifted off balance once again, the same way it did at the beginning of that century.

This has a lot to do with Maastricht. Maastricht is the product of a new ideology, the ideology of europeism, which is a conglomerate of many old non-liberal attitudes. Maastricht is a transition in quality from a community of sovereign European states into a union which stands above individual states and therefore seeks to obtain its mandate and authority from regions or directly from individual citizens.

29

This is a new unification of Europe, considered by its pioneers to be a victory over the fragmented past. The costs and benefits of this unification are not being compared in any serious way: it is assumed instead that costs are zero and benefits are enormous. This assumption should be tested. Political costs and benefits are hard to compare, because we cannot measure them quantitatively, but that does not mean we should not subject them to analysis. Economic costs that can be measured should be analyzed even more.

One important 'cost', or perhaps a threat, is plain to see. Historians have shown us convincingly that fragmentation of Europe – in comparison to other great empires – brought freedom. This clearly implies that the highest guarantee of individual freedom is the democratic nation state, and in that sense a continental union, controlled by one central authority, is an obvious danger. I have no doubt in my mind that the survival of the nation state is a key condition for the survival of a liberal and democratic society.

Maastricht and europeism are the products of non-liberal thought, which unfortunately is not limited only to Socialists and Social Democrats but applies also to Christian Democrats. In 1993 the French (non-socialist) prime minister Balladur, when asked for the definition of the market, said the following memorable words:

> What is the market? It is the law of the jungle, the law of nature. And what is civilization? It is the struggle against nature.

I am afraid there is a broad coalition of people in Europe today who share this kind of thinking and whose concept of Europe is based on such thinking. Under the pretext of eliminating wars and competing with other continents, we see the birth of false internationalism, a free hand for ambitious politicians and the bureaucracy (thanks to the elimination of local political responsibility and accountability) and a new social order.

The European 'president', Romano Prodi, said in November 2011 at the banking forum in Frankfurt: 'Intergovernmentalism (i.e. a community of sovereign states – V.K.) I believe, is a recipe for indecision or, at best, for progress based on the lowest common denominator'. Romano Prodi is therefore telling us that he favours activism from the top, and that he wants to move forward not by the pace of 'the last one in line' who wishes to join, but by the pace of the first in line who comes with the new initiative that all others must accept.[6]

I cannot resist making this update: It is most fascinating how José Barroso, the Prodi of today, uses not similar, but identical words in a speech to the European Parliament on 28 September 2011:

The pace of our endeavors cannot be dictated by the slowest. And today we have a Union where it is the slowest member that dictates the speed of all the other Member States.

6. *Mlada fronta Dnes*, available at www.klaus.cz [6 December 2001].

Barroso makes it clear that it will be necessary to make further radical changes in the Lisbon Treaty, especially to eliminate the principle of unanimous decisions. His arguments are awesome. Whenever a member state brings up the topic of sovereignty, Barroso counters:

> But a Member State does not have the right to block the moves of others, the others also have a national sovereignty and if they want to go further they should go further.[7]

This argument is incredible, but it does affect me – Barroso is my other 'prime minister', next to Petr Nečas, premier of the Czech Republic.

And allow me to make two more brief comments. It is charming to hear Barroso speak of renewal without being able to look back with the least amount of critical analysis. Renewal to him means the Union, ever deeper and deeper. The way forward, towards renewal, is only possible via a deeper Union and everything is measured by the velocity of such motion. That is why

7. 'European renewal: state of the Union speech', Strasbourg, 2011.

some countries are slower in grasping matters correctly. The possibility of thinking differently is excluded completely.

That is what Maastricht was all about. It was the proverbial crossing of the Rubicon, although many steps in this direction had been taken in the years before that. The famous English liberal (and famous commentator on our Velvet Revolution), Timothy Garton Ash, said:

> After all, every previous alliance, coalition, entente, empire, community or monetary union of European states has collapsed sooner or later.[8]

This was true in the past, but is it true today? Maastricht was a big step towards strengthening ties inside Europe, casting them in reinforced concrete if you wish, (so that they do not break up), but nobody wants to hear a single word about the risk involved in the transition from institutions guaranteeing liberalization in Europe (such as the creation of the common

8   (2001), 'The European Orchestra', *Hoover Digest* No. 3.

market on the basis of the Treaty of Rome) towards the European superstate (based on the Maastricht Treaty).

I have no reason to add anything to this text first published ten years ago. I am not able to formulate it any more clearly. That is why I leave it unchanged. The problem is that texts of this sort were ignored for decades, and if there was any response to them, it was by way of ridicule or caricature. They were called 'eurosceptic' in a very authoritarian way and that was enough – there was no need for arguments. Authority was used for delivering the verdict, not the argument. And just to update the historical timeline, three more countries joined the EU on 1 January 1995, namely Finland, Austria and Sweden, taking the number of member countries to 15.

Unfortunately, the Maastricht Treaty was not the end of the European institutional development. The eurocrats knew very well the process was far from being completed. Therefore, a decade later, they mustered up the courage to unveil another radical project – the embodiment and amplification of the ongoing changes in the European constitution, which

35

was meant to signal the birth of a new entity on the map of world politics with the eventual goal of sending the nation states into oblivion.

As far back as 2004, I wrote a passage that I have no reason to change today:

The European constitution (or perhaps more accurately the Treaty Establishing a Constitution for Europe) is a text that is too long and too complex, undecipherable for a mere mortal, a text which is unread, unstudied and therefore in essence not understood, yet it will fundamentally affect the lives of people on the European continent, for whom it will become their supreme constitutional document. It will affect the lives of all of them, both those who dislike it and those who think they can ignore it ... It is a fundamental document, revolutionary in its substance. Its content is extraordinary beyond any doubt, although its significance is being played down constantly by its authors and advocates. For good reasons that make sense to themselves, they do not want others to know how important it really is.

In its essence, this document represents the decisive step away from the Europe of nation-states towards the Europe of one European Superstate. It is a step away from consensual, repeatedly negotiated and reaffirmed cooperation among European states in thousands of individual matters, towards an irrevocable dominance of pan-European authorities and institutions over the national authorities and institutions.

It is a step away from the states as a primal collectivity of people living in Europe, towards the suppression of their sovereignty and the transfer of that sovereignty to supranational units.

It is a step away from the diversity and independence of European nations (from a humbleness towards them), which has thus far not been disputed by anyone or anything, towards an attempt to create a so-far-non-existent, entirely new, common, and therefore as 'homogeneous' as possible, European nation (and with it the common European symbols, emblems and other external attributes).

All of this and much more cannot be denied, even though different 'Europeans' or self-assigned 'owners of Europeanness' have been trying to do so for a long time.

The 'constitutional treaty' submitted for ratification – and there is no doubt that the very use of the word 'constitution' was meant to highlight that this document was and is of crucial importance – was written and pushed through in the member states' governments by those who seek a substantially accelerated unification of the European continent, and who have been striving for this for a number of years or even decades. The arguments used to advocate their stance are old and well-known throughout the twentieth century. And these arguments were deployed not only by people with noble intentions.

The nation state, in the view of these people, is a relic of the sinister, more or less barbarian European past (which had, in their eyes, lasted until the birth of the European integration project in the 1950s), as the main, if not the only, cause of the wars that have plagued the

European continent in its barbarian past, as fertile ground for the recurrent emergence of undemocratic, totalitarian regimes, as a territory too small for decisions about the 'grander issues' of mankind. Last but not least, they see the nation state as a weak counterbalance to the large countries in other continents, labeled as dangerous simply because they lack the enlightened European view of the world that is held by the architects of the European constitutional treaty.

These people, on the contrary, view a pan-European state as the initial stage of an enlightened, problem-free future, master-minded wisely from above, as a guarantee of the absence of wars, as a trustworthy safeguard of freedom, democracy and human rights (until, indeed, the end of time), as the holder of a broad-minded insight and detached point of view, as an effective counterweight to other super-powers, since it is equipped with better ideology and 'superior values'.

The European democrats, of which I hold myself to be one (both a European and a democrat), view this entirely the other way round. For us the nation states are (and have always been) the core of Europe and a guarantee of its good future. Supranational or pan-European institutions and all attempts to gain control over Europe and govern it from one place have always resulted in a lack of freedom, national oppression, subordination to the large and powerful, and similar effects. That is why they were sooner or later abandoned.

The authors of this text, which came into being at the beginning of the promising twenty-first century, know very well that the citizens of the European continent who, on the basis of their own experience and the experience of entire generations of their ancestors, cherish their citizenship and civic rights in the framework of existing nation states, do not want to take this fundamental and, in effect, immense – one might say outright 'Misesian' – step or leap into the unknown.

Therefore they try not to take the citizens' opinion on these things into consideration

– under the pretext that the common people are not yet (and never will be) mature enough to make decisions on such grand issues and that is why they need to be guided by those – the self-appointed vanguard – who matured a long time ago. Much could be written about what is hidden behind their assumptions. It would be possible to write a lot about their real motivation. I do not think their behaviour is caused by any intellectual defect or incapability to think through the different contexts and consequences, which perhaps at first glance are not to be seen if we fail to look carefully enough.

Their behaviour is rather caused by their mistaken opinions, their wrong interpretations of the past, their misunderstandings of key pre-requisites of freedom, democracy and prosperity. They are victims of Hayek's fatal conceit, the misplaced pride of Man and his reasoning.

Their behaviour is also caused, by their very base (although in a certain sense perhaps understandable) interests, their belief that they can assert themselves in today's

41

over-bureaucratized pan-European state
and in its many institutions (which, unlike
the institutions of individual states, have
the privilege that they stand far outside
authentic civic control).

And because they know it well, their 'constitutional treaty' is deliberately unclear,
deliberately diffuse, deliberately incon-
sistent. That is why many things are kept
undercover, unsaid or not fully expounded.
That is why it is not easy to understand
the treaty, and that is why it is particularly
not easy to comprehend all of the effects
it has on the lives of us all. That is why its
text itself is an interim document, which
will need to be followed by others, before
that small, final, and already very clear and
understandable step is taken.[9]

When I conceived this text seven years ago,
I knew the legal arguments related to the
European constitution were too complex and

9. 'Let Us Say YES or NO to the European consti-
    tution', *CEP Praha*, April 2005. Also see *Year Three*
    (2006), Prague: Euromedia.

multi-layered. That is why I tried to simplify them in the 'ten commandments' of what the 'European Constitutional Treaty' will bring:

1. The European Union will become a state and will have all the fundamental features of a state. It will have its own constitution, its citizens, its territory, its external border, its currency, its president, its minister of foreign affairs, etc. It will have its own flag, anthem and public holiday. (Some of these features already exist; others are introduced or strengthened by this document.)

2. In this newly established state of a federalist type, current member states will still be called states, but in reality they will have no more power than mere regions or provinces. The President of the Republic will still be called politely 'Mr. President' by the European bureaucrats, but the 'European directives' will be carried out regardless of the wishes of the people or of their elected representatives in the member states.

3. The constitution of the EU State will be superior to the constitutions of the member states. The entire Union's legal

order will also have primacy over the legal order of the member states.

4. The very term 'constitutional treaty' is imprecise and only temporary. This document will be a treaty between sovereign states only as long as it is not ratified – as a treaty in the member states. Then it will become a real constitution.

5. The concept of shared sovereignty – hitherto dominant in today's old EU – is being weakened and a new pan-European sovereignty is emerging instead. In the new EU the states are definitively losing their hitherto exclusive right to create their own laws.

6. The citizens of the individual member states will become citizens of the State of the European Union, with direct rights and obligations to the institutions of this European State. It is possible to be a citizen of a State; it is not possible to be a citizen of an international organization.

7. The member states will only be able to exercise those competences that are left to them under the EU constitution, not the other way round, which was the original idea of European integration. Derived

(secondary) EU legal acts will be superior to the original (primary) legal acts of the member states. The primary and the secondary are trading places.

8. The EU, not the member states will have the exclusive power to sign most international treaties with other states. The new member states will only be able to sign treaties that will 'unreservedly support the common international and security policy line'.

9. In the voting procedures, the weight of smaller member states, including the Czech Republic, is decreasing with the constitutional treaty (as compared to the current situation resulting from the Treaty of Nice).

10. The Union itself can extend its own sphere of competence through the so-called 'flexibility clause' and 'passerelle clause'. Even those areas of decision-making in which the member states will retain in the future their right of veto can be at any time transferred under majority voting (it is sufficient that the presidents or prime ministers of the EU countries agree on this unanimously, without the national parliaments having to decide on the issue, to say nothing of the citizens' consent).

Two countries dared to hold referenda. Much to the surprise of all eurocrats, the two 'old' founding members of the original six – France and the Netherlands – rejected the European constitution. The eurocrats, however, did not consider this to be an important signal of popular will. It was interpreted as an unqualified decision of ignorant people unprepared for the new situation (calling it *de facto* the failure of the people). Two conclusions were drawn, and both should be a loud warning for the future.[10] And loud warnings they were. American Republican Newt Gingrich, back in 2005, said that a victory over the European constitution is a Pyrrhic victory.

The first conclusion was that there will be no more referendums, because the opinions of people – the voters – amount to an unnecessary nuisance. The second conclusion, a product of lawyers around Angela Merkel, was that people should not be given a relatively

10. These were not the first two controversial plebiscites. The French said a very narrow yes to Maastricht in 1992, the Danes have rejected this document altogether, the Irish turned down the Treaty of Nice in 2001 and the Swedes rejected the euro in 2003.

understandable, coherent, full and straight-forward text of the constitution:[11] instead, the draft should be presented through amendments of previous treaties (that are unintelligible even for experts), with certain words inserted and other sentences left out.

With the exception of formalities, such as the anthem, the flag and similar elements of the already familiar European folklore, the

11. John Laughland describes very convincingly the fact that the declaration of the European constitution was bound to face certain political opposition in his 'European Integration: A Marxist Utopia' ('The Monist', vol. 92, No. 2, 2009). He considers it highly symbolic that 'European leaders quickly realised their mistake and decided ... to return to their old methods, [...] to disguise the key elements of the constitution in a new treaty which was specifically designed to be unclear and indeed incomprehensible to the ordinary voter'. (p. 217). Laughland quotes the well known fact that the president of the European convention set up for the drafting of the constitution, Giscard d'Estaing, confirmed this explicitly in *Le Monde* in October 2007 when he said that the constitutional treaty is included in the Lisbon Treaty 'as a whole, but in a different sequence by way of inserts into previous treaties'.

Constitutional Treaty was rewritten into the
Lisbon Treaty.[12]

A referendum was held in only one country
this time. In Ireland, much to the surprise
of all, the voters turned this intentionally

12. Anthony Coughlan, Irish political scientist and
lawyer offers the most precise analysis in this respect.
I will quote from his brief, yet very consistent text
published in *Today's World (and Václav Klaus)*, a
Festschrift written on the occasion of my birthday, a
text he calls 'The Treaty of Lisbon: A Constitutional
Revolution by Stealth': 'For Lisbon ... establishes
for the first time a European Union constitutionally
separate from and superior to its Member States.
[...] The 27 EU Member States thereby lose their
character as true sovereign states. [...] The Lisbon
treaty changed the situation fundamentally by giving
the post-Lisbon Union the constitutional form of
a true supranational Federation, in other words
a state. [...] This enables the post-Lisbon Union
to function like a state vis-a-vis other states exter-
nally, contracting state treaties and the like, and
in relation to its citizens internally. [...] Lisbon
provided that EU citizenship shall be 'additional
to' national citizenship. [...] The rights and duties
attaching to citizenship of the Union are constitutionally superior to those attaching to one's national
citizenship' (2011, Prague: Fragment, pp. 35–8).

'unintelligible' treaty down. My visit to Ireland at the time and the behavior of Irish eurocratic politicians towards my person were not forgotten by a number of our fellow citizens. I got a clear message from the pro-establishment media, that any criticism of the Lisbon Treaty – rejected by their own voters – was not allowed in Ireland. It is in fact much more sad than it appears: the European Union is no longer the symbol of democracy it pretends to be. The amount of personally-directed hatred and intolerance among those people is fascinating.

The Parliaments of other countries, including the Czech Republic, approved the Lisbon Treaty (the Czech translation was not available at the time of the vote). Only three things were missing to make the document valid after a marathon of negotiations, namely:

1. the repeated Irish referendum, where – after an incredible amount of pressure applied on Irish voters both from inside and outside the country – the treaty was eventually approved.
2. the decision of the German Constitutional Court, confirming that the Treaty of

Lisbon was compliant with the German constitution. The court eventually gave an alibistic verdict, making the approval *de facto* conditional (which Chancellor Merkel immediately interpreted as sufficient).

3. my signature, which was the last to be added, following dramatic deliberations of the Czech Constitutional Court, with whose conclusions I beg to differ. I could have held out, but the political significance of such a gesture would have been limited. I should most probably have been 'banished' from the political scene and one more dissenting voice would have been silenced.

I can make mistakes, and that is why I take seriously the opinions of those who were disappointed and contacted me *en masse* after my signature appeared under the Lisbon Treaty. Some even compared it to what president Beneš did in the years 1938 and 1948. However, I neither flew to England to emigrate, nor resigned as President. For all those who were disappointed, I will name Ladislav Jakl, author of the article 'Lisbon Is Gone, the Conflict of Visions Remains', who argues that I should have been tougher in my opposition to Lisbon, that I should have come up with tougher conditions for my signature and that perhaps I should even have tried to block the ratification altogether.

I think L. Jakl is right in concluding that my long battle, which ended in defeat, was perhaps not fought in vain:

> The euro-centralizers got the message that their position could be increasingly difficult in time. Every grain of sand thrown into the ruthless works of the centralizing euroma-chinery is an investment into the future.[13]

When commenting on the decision of the Constitutional Court, Jakl said:

> One episode of the great conflict is over. But the conflict is permanent. It is a conflict between the advocates of freedom and those who say that all methods can be used when enforcement of The Good is at stake.[14]

13. Jakl, Ladislav (November 2009), 'Lisbon is gone, the conflict of visions remains', *CEP Newsletter*, p. 2.
14. Ibid., p. 3.

51

I communicated with the Constitutional Court twice in this context, having been asked by the Court to do so. The first time was in June 2008.[15] I welcomed the Senate's petition to assess the compliance of the Lisbon Treaty and I identified myself with it. To put things into perspective, I remind the reader that I was already in an explicit disagreement with the EU Charter of Rights, as proven in point 4.2 of my argument:

The EU Charter of Rights is a useless document in itself. Member States have their own charters of rights, which are usually much better prepared. At the international level, human rights and freedoms are guaranteed by the European Convention for the Protection of Human Rights and Fundamental Freedoms of the Council of

15. 'Reply to the Constitutional Court regarding the Lisbon Treaty' was a response to the proposal of the Senate of the Czech Republic, filing a petition to assess the compliance of the Lisbon Treaty. The reply (which I will call in this text Reply I) was handed over to the Constitutional Court on 3 June, 2008. See www.klaus.cz/clanky/850 and *Year Six*, (2009), Prague: Euromedia.

Europe, and its Additional Protocols. It has been tested by history and, in particular, has a functional mechanism of court control available (in contrast to the EU Charter of Rights). This means that the EU Charter of Rights makes sense only if the EU considers itself to be a State *sui generis* or an emerging State of a federal type, which is subsequently bound by international law to observe and protect human rights.

Some may remember that after ratifying the Lisbon Treaty I asked for the so-called opt-out which would separate the EU Charter of Rights from the Lisbon Treaty. This was very precisely described by Jiří Weigl in his article 'The Lisbon Opt-Out and Other Related Matters'.[16]

It is good to remind ourselves, after all those years and in the atmosphere of general forgetfulness, that Topolánek's government, formulating its mandate for negotiating the Lisbon Treaty in 2007, asked to seek the same opt-out that I eventually sought two years

16. *CEP Newsletter*, November 2009.

later. Nobody acknowledged this in 2009 and nobody does so even now. This was no original move and I was not alone in making it. I was well aware – and most certainly in 2007 the Czech government shared this position – that this charter would lead to much uncertainty, depending on how the EU Court of Justice in Luxembourg would interpret the individual paragraphs and especially how they would be applied in legal practice. My focus was on property issues and how they would be interpreted in the suits filed by the Sudeten Germans, who had been transferred from the Czech Republic to Germany after World War II. This is a crucial issue in our history and I vehemently reject its belittlement by advocates of europeism and globalization, who gave up on the nation state a long time ago anyway.

It is good to see that a similar opt-out was negotiated by Great Britain and Poland. Britain focused on the charter's maximalistic concept of social rights, while conservative, Catholic Poland was alarmed by the unacceptability of various fashionable progressivistic quasi-rights.

My request for an opt-out was approved by the European Council at its session of 29–30 October 2009. The only question now is whether we will remain united, and Jiří Weigl also mentions this in the article I have already quoted from. Despite the opposition of the Senate, the situation now, in October 2011, seems hopeful.

I was explicit in expressing my opinion on the symbolic differences between a European constitution and the Lisbon Treaty in point 4.5 of Reply I:

> In view of the aforementioned facts, it is *de iure* absolutely insignificant that the Lisbon Treaty eventually does not codify European symbols – a flag, an anthem, and a motto. Symbols are not among the essential hallmarks of a state according to international law. They are also not exclusive symbols of states: associations and nongovernmental organizations of various kinds usually have their symbols as well. Moreover, European symbols have been in place for a long time and will certainly continue to exist on the basis of international custom, that is, the so-called secondary law of the

55

EU. Therefore, it cannot be stated that the omission of symbols fundamentally distinguishes the Lisbon Treaty from the rejected draft European Constitution. The only difference between them is in their form: while the EU Constitution replaces the existing agreements, the Lisbon Treaty is drafted in such a way that it amends them, thus making the so-called primary law of the EU even less transparent than it is now.

At the end of my letter I demanded explicit answers to five fundamental questions:

Question One:
Will the Czech Republic remain a sovereign country and a full-fledged entity of the international community, capable of adhering to the obligations arising for it from international law, even after the Lisbon Treaty enters into force?

Question Two:
Does the provision of the Lisbon Treaty concerning the internal effect of EU legislation comply with Article 10 of the Constitution of the Czech Republic?

Question Three:
Does the EU Charter of Fundamental Rights have the legal status of an international treaty according to Article 10a and/or Article 10 of the Constitution; if so, do all of its provisions comply with the Charter of Fundamental Rights and Freedoms of the Czech Republic and/or other parts of the constitutional system?

Question Four:
Will the European Union remain an international organization or institution to which Article 10a of the Constitution allows the transfer of powers of the bodies of the Czech Republic after the Lisbon Treaty enters into force?

Question Five:
If the Lisbon Treaty amends, albeit indirectly, the Accession Treaty, does Constitutional Act No 515/2002 Coll. on the Referendum on the Czech Republic's Accession to the European Union not implicitly apply to the Lisbon Treaty as well (if so, it would be necessary to amend, in particular, the referendum question)? Then,

should the approval of the ratification of the Lisbon Treaty not be subject to a referendum as well?

There was no way I could have been satisfied with the finding of the Constitutional Court, because it was both undignified and beside the point. A year later I was asked by the Constitutional Court for further explanation, this time responding to the petition of a group of senators who had used new arguments to ask new questions on the same issue. My reply of 16 October 2009, let us call it Reply II,[17] summed up my arguments and emphasized the following:

The Constitutional Court is therefore deciding on a matter that is absolutely fundamental for the future of our country. It is deciding the future of a state, for the sovereignty of which previous generations fought in both world wars, the sovereignty that was later taken away from us by the communist totalitarian regime. Twenty

17. See www.klaus.cz/clanky/1141 and *Year Seven* (2010), Prague: Euromedia.

years after restoring our democracy and sovereignty, we are once again dealing with the question whether we should – this time voluntarily, based on our free will – give up the position of a sovereign state and hand over decison-making on our own matters to European institutions that are outside the democratic control of our citizens.

I also said:

I am fully aware that the deliberation of the Constitutional Court is taking place at a time when the Czech Republic is exposed to extraordinary pressure, both from some domestic circles and from abroad. I am confident these external pressures will not affect the court's decision. Similarly, the results of the ratification processes in other countries of the European Union must not have any impact on the Court's decision, because here the Czech Constitutional Court is assessing the compliance of the Lisbon Treaty with the Constitution of the Czech Republic. It is also necessary to point out that the Constitutional Court is not assessing the compliance of the Constitution with the Lisbon Treaty: instead, it is assessing the compliance of the Lisbon Treaty with the Constitution.

I concluded the relatively long and detailed text with these words:

I disagree with those saying speedy ratification of the Lisbon Treaty is necessary without a clear and full elimination of all the doubts, that are still felt by constitutional dignitaries as well as by the general public after the finding of the Constitutional Court of 26 October 2008. The fact that the Lisbon Treaty is a document which will have fundamental consequences both inside the country and in international relations is obvious and well illustrated by the lengthy ratification processes in individual member countries of the EU. These processes were accompanied by a number of problems and complications. In some countries, opt-outs and exceptions were needed to complete ratification. When such a fundamental international treaty is at stake, many questions have to be answered – questions that have to do with the Treaty itself as well as the circumstances and context in which it was drafted and in which it might become valid in the Czech Republic and other EU countries.

Therefore, as a participant in proceedings on a complaint filed by a group of senators requesting an assessment of compliance of the Lisbon Treaty, I suggest amending the Treaty on the European Union and the Treaty Establishing the European Community, and/or its selected provisions with the constitutional system, and I ask the Constitutional Court to make a clear and concrete ruling with detailed justification on the question whether the Lisbon Treaty as a whole complies with article 1, paragraph 1 of the Constitution of the Czech Republic and/or article 2, paragraph 1 of the Charter of Fundamental Rights and Freedoms, and to state whether the Czech Republic will remain a sovereign, unified and democratic state under a rule of law based on respect for the rights and freedoms of man after the ratification of the Lisbon Treaty.

As we know, the Constitutional Court decided, on the basis of a dubious argument about the so-called material core of the Constitution of the Czech Republic, that the petition of a group of senators was invalid. To complete my historical outline, which becomes a pre-historic outline given the current Greek crisis, let me say that the EU accepted ten more members in 2004, adding Bulgaria and Romania in 2007.

The euro, the common currency for 17 member countries of the EU, came into effect. It did not work for long. The debt crisis started in the spring of 2010. More about this later.

TWO

The inherent instability of the current interim phase

As the institutional framework evolved in the course of European integration – from the EEC via the EC to the EU – to use the language of acronyms – it took a decade to reach a phase, or rather an interim phase, known as the European Monetary Union or EMU.

Even if European politicians in the 1990s did not realize this well enough, much less the European public, this is a qualitative shift, a new phase with new and specific characteristics, placing new demands on member countries.

It is no revelation, and it requires no courage to say it today, that many in Europe underestimated the difficulties arising in this phase. Almost everybody recognizes them now.

The expression 'interim phase' is probably accurate, too, because it is obvious at first sight that an unstable system was created, which either has to return to the EU (it is potentially possible that the EMU will survive, but with a much smaller number of more homogeneous countries), or it will have to evolve smoothly into the EFU, the European

Fiscal (or Financial) Union, and then – sooner or later – into the final phase: the EPU, the European Political Union[1], even if the politicians in Brussels will probably insist on using the old EU abbreviation.

I hope the reader understands I am using the acronyms EPU as well as EFU as analytical terms, with no ambition to cast a new official name for the future European supranational grouping. (I almost feel like adding the acronym ESU, the European Social Union, a term used by H.-W. Sinn in his paper 'Der kranke Mann Europas'[2]. A decade ago, he was referring to Germany, not to Greece, but times change quickly!)

The European Union of today – especially because of the shift from EU to EMU – is in an obvious crisis, even if the eurocrats deny it. This crisis did not come in 2010 – in connection with the problems in Greece – not even several

1. I used this acronym for the first time in December 1998 in Luxembourg, several days before the first phase of the euro (cashless, transferable euro) became effective.
2. IFO Institute, Munich, 15 November 2003.

years before that, in connection with the euro-American (or US-European) financial and economic crisis. It was self-evident long before that when Europe was in a period of stagnation, accompanied by various economic problems. Economic growth in the EU throughout the first decade of the twenty-first century was the slowest since the 1950s, even if nobody wants to admit it.[3]

I fully agree with Professor Petr Fiala from the Masaryk University, who says that 'people knew something was wrong' and that they knew it 'before the economic downturn appeared' and way before the 'beginning of the eurozone crisis'.[4]

The only question is whether the EU and its politicians will admit to themselves how deep, serious and inevitable this crisis is (and that

3. Perhaps we could accept the argument that the post-war reconstruction of Europe in ruins allowed for an excessively fast, but unsustainable growth, but that is no argument for each following decade to show ever slower growth.
4. In his article 'Europe and the Weakening of the Occident', *Kontexty*, No. 4, 2011, p. 6.

it is not an economic, much less a financial crisis) and start acting accordingly, or whether the current status-quo continues, based on the idea that nothing serious is happening, that a few cosmetic changes will be enough to take care of the problem, that the solution is to start up economic growth using an unknown triggering mechanism, that we will 'grow up from the crisis' and, therefore, that no substantial actions are needed, that we can keep on overregulating human activities despite the obvious retardation and paralysis, that we can allow ourselves to be drawn by the Greens or environmentalists into economically non-feasible projects, and that we can give the Greens (hidden in political parties from left to right) ever greater powers in public decisions – which is what is happening right now at an accelerating pace – and that we can press on for more and more projects for which we do not have the necessary finances, just because they are listed in various 'charters' with noble names (this time I mean projects that are more red and orange rather than green).

Everything seems to indicate that this is where Europe is going. Ordinary people have known for some time that it was essential to be resolute in making changes, including a 'critical mass' of reforms, but the politicians, surrounded by their bureaucracy and public intellectuals, irresponsible by the very definiton of their position, together with the self-confident and irresponsible media, will spare no means to prevent fundamental change, because such change is contrary to their vested interests. They love the status quo.

In my article 'Let us create a different European Union', quoted at the beginning, I said in 2005:

> Political elites have always known that the shift in decision-making from the national to the supranational level weakens the traditional democratic mechanisms (that are inseparable from the existence of a nation state) and this increases their power in a radical way. This is why they wanted this shift so badly in the past, and that is why they want it today.

Together, they have formed a mighty coalition which – and yes, I forgot to mention the scientists and artists, recipients of generous grants, often from the EU – will block such change. I take part in European debates at least once a week in various parts of our continent and I am a first-hand eyewitness in that respect.

The question is whether the current apolitical European configuration allows such change.[5] Do we have real politics in Europe today – the

5. John Laughland says in the earlier quoted article, that since the times of Jean Monnet 'in all cases, the view is that politics is itself a cause of conflict and that the path to peace therefore lies in depoliti- cisation or antipolitics' (op. cit., p. 215). These opinions – exclusively European at first, but now adopted also by Americans – assume that 'politics can be dissipated away into administration'. This brings Laughland to the conclusion that the EU is not building a superstate, but a non-state, that the 'deconstruction of the state' is being carried out, implementing the old marxist utopia. Marx, in his book *The Poverty of Philosophy* considers the state to be a 'historical and transitory product', and formu- lates his theory of the 'withering state'. The famous words of John Fitzgerald Kennedy spoken in 1962 that 'modern problems are primarily technical rather than political and far beyond the comprehension of most men' seem to indicate that the architects of European integration were not alone in their thinking.

political conflict of opinions – or have real politics been in fact eliminated by reducing the weight and importance of the nation states and by the self-confessed apolitical ways of Brussels? Is this irreversible? Has the chance for any systemic change been eliminated together with politics? I am not too optimistic.

Change will not come from within the institutions in Brussels. I am afraid the only way of returning to actual political activity would be a wave of political discontent in some large European state. I do not expect this to happen in Spain, France or Italy, but even in Germany or Great Britain I do not see politicians and political parties that would want such change. And the small countries do not have the necessary power, even if they had such politicians.

The present interim phase can – for exclusively economic reasons – survive for a limited period of time, but only at the cost of stagnation and economic retardation. Europe will inevitably fall behind the rest of the world. Communism also managed to survive stagnation long enough. But there can be other shocks involved – the sudden disintegration of elementary social cohesion in individual European countries, thanks to the multicultural apotheosis of immigration and of minorities, both having the same explosive potential. Such shocks can be much more destructive than gradual economic disintegration. Do not let me be misunderstood, I am not talking about the invasion of the new barbarians (they are called Islamic fundamentalists today). By the way, in contradiction to traditional historical views, the barbarians did not cause the fall of the Roman Empire. It destroyed itself, from within through weakness, loss of social coherence, loss of the system of values on which it was founded and which kept it going, whether they knew it or not.[6]

6. This is the argument of Jonathan Sacks, who tries to determine why the greatest civilizations eventually fall: 'The reason they do so is not necessarily the rise of a stronger power. It is their own internal decay... The challenge was the underlying moral health of Western liberal democracies ... their sense of identity and collective responsibility, their commitment to one another and to the ideals that brought them into being'. He sees Europe as 'a chimera of societies without a shared moral code, nations without a

In the latter half of September 2011, I was in New York, attending a dinner given by *The New Criterion* magazine, where I was asked time and again about the eurozone crisis. I tried to explain the context by saying that the eurozone crisis is only the tip of the iceberg, that in fact the problems are much broader and deeper. But I stuck to the economic and political dimension of the question, I spoke about the democratic deficit in the design of European integration, the various defects of the European economic system (in accepting the social-market economic model with a strong ecological aspect), and one senior American participant asked me this question: Is it not all caused by the defect of the European system of values? Is it not caused by the extreme seculari-zation of European society since the time of the French revolution? Should we not look for the culprit further than Monnet, Schuman, Delors or Barroso? Is it not Jean-Jacques Rousseau after all? All I could do was to agree with him.

collective identity, cultures without a respect for tradition, groups without a concern for the common good, and politics without the slightest sense of history'. ('How to Reverse the West's Decline', Standpoint, September 2011, pp. 42–3).

The topic of their conference was *Is America Declining?* The speakers did not shy away from criticizing many of America's recent administrations. They were looking at a much broader context. And I am convinced they were right in doing so.

But I do not wish to devote this text to this topic. What I am trying to explain in the broader sense is something I hinted at in my speech in Stará Boleslav in September 2011[7] on the occasion of the St. Wenceslas pilgrimage. I will repeat again that this is what the small-minded and typically Czech dispute around Mr. Bátora[8] is all about. If some of us – even from allegedly rightist political parties – do not want to understand it, it is sad.

7. 'The speech of the President of the Republic at the National St. Wenceslas Pilgrimage', Lidove noviny, 29 September 2011. Available at www.klaus.cz.
8. Ladislav Bátora worked as head of the Czech Education Ministry's personnel section in 2011 and left the post after a big campaign led by the media, non-governmental organizations and one of the parties in the coalition government which falsely accused him of extremism, anti-Semitism and racism.

I am of the opinion that the problems of European integration, as well as the problems of the European social and economic model, cannot be solved without discussing these broader questions. However, I will refrain from doing so for now, to make the structure of this text more rational. I know about them but I will leave them aside for the moment.

The role of Greece

The Greek example is very illustrative, although I keep repeating that Greece is the cause of neither the present European crisis nor the general debt crisis of the eurozone. Greece cannot even be blamed for joining the eurozone – which is what some say with cheap, albeit fashionable criticism. Greece not only joined the eurozone, she was also accepted as a member. The blame lies therefore on both sides. It is equally true that Greece borrowed too much money, but on the other hand there were those who provided the excessive (and irresponsible) loans. Greece should, though, accept criticism even from politicians in friendly countries.

Greece is not the first country undergoing an enormous financial crisis. We remember the unfortunate Argentinian experience brought about by similar currency problems. Many countries in history went bankrupt. As long ago as 1742 David Hume, in his book *On Public Credit*, said:

> It would scarcely be more imprudent to give a prodigal son a credit in every banker's shop in London, than to impower a statesman to draw bills, in this manner, upon posterity.

Economists know well that financial crises are followed by states going bankrupt. In the words of Niall Ferguson (in his John Bonython Lecture delivered in Sydney, Australia last year): 'The most obvious point is that imperial falls are associated with fiscal crises ...'

The weakest link is inevitably found every time. Greece has a unique, ancient past, but she has not fared well in recent times. In the last two centuries the country was alternately under the regime of the Ottoman Empire, a kingdom, a dictatorship and now a democracy.

The nation's public finances were as unstable as its politics during that time.

Greece first defaulted on her debts in 1826 and then once again in 1932. For half of the last two centuries she was either in default or restructuring her public finances. She entered the twenty-first century with a debt amounting to 90 per cent of GDP, the third highest proportional debt among the 30 countries in the OECD. Between 1995 and 2008 (that is before the financial and economic crisis) her budget deficit limit of 4 per cent of GDP was exceeded ten times (in 2004, the year of the Olympics in Athens the state budget deficit was at 7.4 per cent, which is a good thing to remember when we consider having the Olympics in Prague). In 2010, the Greek debt amounted to 140 per cent of GDP, second only to Japan.

Michael Massourakis, chief economist in one of Greece's biggest financial institutions, the Alpha Bank, offers a telling description of the Greek situation in his article 'Greece and the State' (*World Economics Quarterly*, No. 2, 2010). He reminds us, among other things, of the fact that 'Greece was the only EU country that adopted the euro with a two-year delay, as Greeks were not ready at the prescribed time'.[9]

Greece adopted the euro in 2001. The cause of the problem, according to Massourakis, was the excessively dominant role of the state in the country's economy. The condemnation of his own country is extremely harsh:

> I intend to tell a story of recklessness, of how distorted and rigid an economy can become by maximizing the benefits for insiders, rent seekers and others who align the state to their service with scant, if any, regard for the rest of the population or future generations ...[10]

He provides a lot of data. I had no idea that according to a World Bank survey Greece ranked 109th – Europe's worst – on the ease of 'doing business' index. According to analysts of the World Forum in Davos, Greece ranks 71st in competitiveness (again using data from

9. Massourakis, Michael (2010), 'Greece and the State', *World Economics Quarterly*, No. 2, p. 45.
10. Ibid., p. 48.

2010). And, as I have already said, all this is possible, but it is not possible to be in a currency union with Germany at the same time. Or perhaps even that is possible, but it would require the introduction of the same rules and legislation as in Germany. In other words, to become the former German Democratic Republic.

Greece is solvent today only thanks to the loan of €110 billion from the EU and the IMF in May 2010 and thanks to another bailout package of about the same size from the EU in June 2011. The problem started when Greece – after entering the eurozone – got access to excessive and cheap loans at interest rates as low as those enjoyed by the healthy countries of the eurozone, i.e. rates much lower than she had had to pay before she adopted the euro in 2001. Underestimation of Greece's debt risk was quite common around the world before the global financial crisis of 2008. In 2003, when the deficit in Greek government spending was at 6 per cent of GDP, all the main rating agencies gave Greece a very decent A plus. Greece maintained this rating until one month before the moment when she sought help from the IMF in 2010. This is just a complementary thought on the broader question of who is to blame. Let me say again that Greece was not alone in this.

No clear warnings were given by the EU, OECD or the IMF throughout the period of permanent deficit in the Greek finances. I agree with Adam Creighton, who says that 'Some lenders had reason to think European governments and intergovernmental agencies would "bail out" Greece (and therefore bondholders) if it proved unable to repay its debts'.[11]

This is precisely what owners of the Greek debt thought.

It is time to say clearly that the current Greek and indeed European problem runs much deeper. Milton Ezrati anticipates that what we see today is just the beginning. He says

11. Creighton, Adam, (Spring 2011), 'Greece's Debt Crisis – the Price of Cheap Loans', *Policy Magazine*, Vol. 27, No. 3, p. 12.

'Today's problems ... lie in the basic structure of the euro'.[12]

This is the same argument as the one we hear from Creighton: 'The Greek debt crisis has resulted from confusion about the nature of the European Union'.[13]

This fact is complicated by similar problems that had occurred in Ireland by the end of 2010 (Ireland has received €85 billion in aid from the EU so far) and in Portugal in the spring of 2011 (she got a promise of €78 billion). In the meantime the Greek debt keeps growing and is expected to reach 160 per cent of GDP. Given the planned deficit budget deficit of 8 per cent of GDP, it is clear that, while GDP is still going down, the debt-to-GDP ratio will go up. That is elementary arithmetic. Today, Greece has to pay an interest rate of 15.5 per cent on a ten-year government bond and 23 per cent on a two-year bond, damaging her financial situation severely. It is obvious that taxpayers

12. Ezrati, Milton, (Summer 2011) 'Only the Beginning', *The International Economy,* p. 71.
13. Creighton, Op. cit. p. 14.

in Europe will have to bear the immediate burden of the loans from various state organizations as well as those who have provided the irresponsible loans in the past, especially the banks whose solvency may thus be in danger. I do not want even to think about what would happen should a large country like Italy have similar problems with its current debt of 120 per cent of GDP. There would be no good solution there.

The culprit here is the euro, which was wrongly constructed from the outset. Adoption of the euro not only made it possible for all member countries – very different in their fiscal behavior – to borrow with the same interest rate. One exchange rate cannot be beneficial to all, especially for countries that joined the eurozone with widely different exchange rates inherited from their former national currencies.

M. Ezrati is precisely right in saying:

> When Greece and much of the rest of Europe's periphery joined the euro, they exchanged their national currencies at higher rates than their economic fundamentals of

productivity and profitability could justify. In contrast, when Germany joined, it made the exchange at a much lower rate than its economic fundamentals demanded.[14]

The conclusions are quite obvious. After joining the eurozone, the Germans got an advantage from easier exports (this explains the German export boom throughout the last decade), while implicitly lowering the Germans' 'income', which led to higher savings.

Greece and other 'peripheral countries' (I know this expression used by economic analysts today is pretty harsh) were on the opposite side of the deal. The high exchange rate damaged their exporters and the increased purchasing power strengthened the feeling of wealth and prosperity, leading to higher consumption, borrowing and imports.

As a result, Germany and some other countries were saving money, exporting and investing, thus increasing their competitiveness, while other countries were becoming increasingly

14. Ezrati, op. cit., p. 73.

dependent on imports, paying no attention to productivity, further undercutting their competitiveness.

This proves again the trivial fact that the rate of exchange is a fundamental economic parameter, a key price signal. If all the countries of the European 'periphery' still had their drachmas, the solution would be easy, and in fact such discrepancies could never occur. Because they do not have their drachmas any more, they have to set out on a long and painful road towards adjustment, different from a simple adjustment of the exchange rate – through deflation or at least much lower inflation than in Germany and other strong economies of the EU.

Economists know well that relative changes of prices and income have the same effect as revaluation and devaluation. They also know that this adjustment will take a longer time, while various bailout packages will have to be the interim solution. The debate in Europe today and tomorrow will only be about who is to pay for this 'solidarity', whether it should be the taxpayers (the states), or the creditors, who made a bad investment decision by buying supposedly 'sovereign' junk bonds.

The failure of these investors, banks and other financial institutions is obvious. Assessing the creditworthiness of their clients is the banks' main business, whether the debtors are private institutions or states. If the problems do not spill over into other countries, and if the European banks – and this concerns mostly banks in Germany and France – have enough liquidity to cover their part of the Greek losses, this is no fatal danger for them. They should not be allowed to convince us, though, that it is they who should be protected and saved. Under the condition of the generous solution used in the preceding US financial crisis – as well as in Europe – the banks' bailout was a little too sweet and they may be counting on somebody else paying for their losses again.

As I said above, the interim phase of the EMU is an unstable system and the current European debt crisis proves it perfectly. Greece is 'merely' the most visible example of a more general problem.

THREE

The economic benefits of territorial integration: too much optimism?

Creating a larger economic area, or expanding the market, is an undisputable economic benefit, although – as everything else in human life – it may sometimes be relative only. Opening up, liberalization, elimination of cross-border barriers of all kinds, free movement of goods and services, people and money (but also of ideas and cultural patterns) allows (and to some extent compels) the division of labour and specialization. It brings economies of scale and creates positive externalities. It is essentially a positive phenomenon in all of these cases, but again only to a certain extent. This is the standard economic thinking on European economic integration.

It is equally well known, that with the growing size of the institutionally linked territory, the problem of 'governability' arises, together with the growing heterogeneity of this large territory. Less than a decade ago, the frequently quoted book by Albert Alesina and Enrik Spolaore, *The Size of Nations*[1] tried to find the optimum point between benefits from a larger scale and the costs of heterogeneity. The conclusions drawn

1. (2003), Cambridge: MIT Press.

by both authors were not unequivocal and they did not support the simplistic europeist doctrine very much.

Many of us know very well – to paraphrase the title of Schumacher's book from 1973 – that 'big is not always beautiful'. There are extremely successful and prosperous small countries (from Singapore to Switzerland) and historically there were many dysfunctional large empires, too. There is not and has never been any firm correlation between economic performance and the size of a political entity. Maybe the famous *Small Is Beautiful* is closer to being true, or perhaps we could put it more precisely: the more decentralized the entity is, the better. Economic opening up to the flows of capital and trade is not the same thing as enlarging the size of an administrative entity.

Understanding this, we must ask the question whether the evolution of European integration in the last 50 years was opening up the continent's economy, or whether it was closer to an administrative unification of the original small entities, the nation states. It is not a simple question, given the complex European reality, and it may be easier to ask what was the prevailing tendency in individual historical periods. I am convinced that at the beginning of the European integration in the 1950s, the first tendency prevailed – the opening up, liberalization of all kinds of movements and cross-border flows of 'commodities' (in the most general sense, not limited to economic commodities only) under European institutions which did not have excessive regulatory and dirigistic ambitions, or obligations.

Creating a free-trade zone or a customs union is not a big institutional or organizational problem. Our experience in that respect is clear. No central administration was needed for the functioning of the Central European Free Trade Agreement (CEFTA), which relatively successfully facilitated trade among countries of the Visegrád Four (and was later expanded into other neighbouring countries). Issues that needed decisions were tabled in meetings of ministers for economy, industry or trade and there was no palace built in Brussels or anywhere else. The Visegrád Four has no administrative centre until this day. The meeting of its presidents in October 2011 confirmed the obvious

91

fact that the agenda is drafted by the offices of all four presidents and at the last meeting one president offers to organize the next meeting and asks his three colleagues for topics for discussion.

The first phase of European integration was an economic benefit – because it had economic ambitions. In the second phase, the 'opening up' included other areas than just the flow of commodities, but – although slowly and cautiously, yet quite obviously – the vast bureaucracy in Brussels started growing and – for the sake of its very existence – could not remain idle. It had to initiate massive interventions, regulations and controls, producing an increasing number of directives. It was based on a false, anti-liberal idea that a larger area needs more regulation, although we – educated by Hayek and our communist past – know very well that a larger area (and complexity) needs more market forces and more decentralized decision-making, not the other way around. This is a canonical conclusion.

The socialist-leaning vision – in this case the Franco-German vision, or, using a different terminology the vision of Colbert and the Christian Democrats – managed to enforce regulation, harmonization, standardization, and masterminding of markets at all levels including the pan-European level, on a scale that would not be politically accepted in individual countries, because these still had their own politics.

Ondřej Krutílek, a Czech author, says:

> The EU evolved from a more or less inferior position of an international organization in the hands of the member states into a largely independent entity equipped with a number of defensive mechanisms against its members ... While the European Community was asked to do jobs for its member countries, in the present EU it is often the other way around.[2]

This is a typical 'agent–principal' relationship: the 'agent' (EU) became the principal and the principals (member states) became the 'agents'.

2. Krutílek, Ondřej (2011), 'Deepening of European Integration Is a Fatal Mistake', *Revue Politika*, No. 9.

These relations have been subject to economic theory for a long time. Political scientists use different, but equally productive terminology.

I will take the liberty to formulate a thesis, that European integration, based in principle on a non-liberal view of the world, has already exhausted its liberalizing potential. (It does not desire liberalization and, for ideological reasons, is not even capable of carrying it out). For that reason we see the beginning of the prevalence – and dominance in their effects – of various regulatory, anti-market elements which do not strengthen the economy, but weaken it instead.

There are precious few economic activities with a continental dimension (although some people think the opposite is true) and the assumption that they have to be regulated from some central point is completely false. Similarly, there are very few continental 'public goods'. It is equally wrong to see negative external-ities only – positive externalities outnumber negative externalities in any economy – but it is even more important to see that reality is in fact dominated by positive 'internalities'.

These three points should be explained by economists to the politicians. If that is not so, it is only logical, that eurocrats use these economically well-defined terms very loosely (and successfully among laymen), but certainly not correctly:

- the hypothesis on a continental dimension for a large number of economic activities;
- the hypothesis on a large number of public goods on the continental level, i.e. public goods for which the dimension of a community, city, region, state or a number of states, is not sufficient;
- the hypothesis on the dominance of externalities, especially the negative ones (as opposed to 'internalities' to use my terminology) in any economic activity.

We can add to this argument – using the economic jargon – that when it comes to integrating, there is the merciless law of decreasing marginal benefits, when more does not bring more, but on the contrary after crossing a certain limit it brings nothing, if not less. It is convenient to have the same weights and measures and road signs, but it does not make sense to dictate what kinds of cheese or beer can be produced or how long a dish can remain in a kitchen after it was cooked. It is obvious today, that these useless regulations and directives affect our lives to an astonishing extent, with a new regulation issued virtually every day. O. Krutilek says in the quoted article that over the first seven years of our EU membership (from 1 May 2004 to 5 September 2011, when his article was written) an unprecedented total of 4527 decrees, 686 directives and 6617 decisions were adopted on the European Union's institutional level! I am afraid our citizens do not have the slightest idea about the extent of this interference of Brussels in our domestic affairs.

The question whether an open market (united, in this sense) needs a unified currency is a specific one in this context. There is no doubt that one currency makes transactions easier, or that transaction costs are lowered, in the parlance of economists, but – as always – under certain conditions only. These conditions were formulated by Robert Mundell in his famous article written 50 years ago, 'A Theory of Optimum Currency Areas'.[3]

These conditions were amended and developed in various ways over the years, but they are intuitively easy to understand in their essence: the economic area suitable for one currency must be homogeneous (a trivial but unattainable condition); it must have prices and wages that are flexible and able to adjust in both directions; and there must be a high degree of mobility for production factors such as the labour force and capital. Neither the EU nor the 17 countries of the eurozone today, are such an optimum currency zone. It is a trivial conclusion, but one that is still not appreciated, especially by European politicians. Nevertheless it does have its consequences, of which the most visible is the depth of the current European crisis.

Mundell's conditions for an optimal currency union, similarly to other lines of economic thinking, often remain on the level of merely facilitating transactions. Again, an obvious

3. *American Economic Review*, No. 4, November 1961.

conclusion, certainly truthful, but its quantitative dimension remains a question. How much is that small benefit worth when set against the costs? Is the ease-of-transaction benefit 0.1 per cent of GDP, is it 0.5 per cent, 1 per cent or 10 per cent? Or is it perhaps even less than 0.1 per cent? This question is important, especially since we are living in the age of fast and simple electronic banking transactions and easy-to-use credit and debit cards. This is a highly empirical question, one that defies an easy verdict. Economists do not live in a world of controllable experiments. They are unable to guarantee the condition of *ceteris paribus*.

It is unlikely that the ease-of-transaction benefit will be large. This benefit is offset by various costs. How much does a country stand to lose, should its exchange rate be not precisely in line with its economic parameters? The larger the discrepancy, the larger the loss. It is obvious that this cost can more than nullify the ease-of-transaction benefit.

How many countries are losing money, just because their exchange and interest rates are not tailored precisely to their needs? What was the effect of the inadequately low interest rates Greece had, after it joined the eurozone?

The adoption of a common currency does not have the same flat effect on all countries, much less on their 'insides'. The result is an asymmetric development of individual regions, forcing the state to intervene.

The adoption of a common currency makes inter-state transfers necessary, and that is the key issue in the eurozone today.

Martin Feldstein argues persistently that a country without its own currency does not receive necessary signals from the market. There is no point in repeating that Greece was not getting those signals throughout the last decade.

This does not mean that the current debt crisis of the eurozone is a random episode. This crisis was bound to come. Many knew it would come, sooner or later. The truth is that a common currency is not a necessary or even a desirable precondition for an effectively linked market. The market is automatically 'linked' thanks to the flexibility of prices and wages as well as the mobility of production factors. Also, markets with different currencies are 'linked' by flexible exchange rates (it is more difficult where exchange rates are fixed or semi-fixed). The exchange rate is one of the key economic variables, it provides signals whose forcible elimination inside the eurozone causes huge problems. We know it not only from theory, but we see it with our own eyes, too.

There are more than enough examples of an economically unjustified and therefore problematic unification of currencies. The political unification of Italy 150 years ago, abolishing the conversion mechanism – the exchange rate – between the north and the south, destroyed the opportunity to create a united economy for Italy and as a result, this highly heterogeneous economy was kept in tension for one and a half centuries.

The unification of Germany two decades ago (abolishing the exchange rate between east and west) did not bring about sufficient homogeneity in both parts of Germany to allow the common currency to exist without fiscal transfers on a scale unprecedented in history. (Those transfers were similar in size to the annual GDP of the Czech Republic,[4] which is something that we do not see in Italy or the EU today.)

I know very well that the reason for the division (or anti-unification) of Czechoslovakia at the beginning of the 1990s was both that Slovakia wanted it, and that there had been a loss of solidarity on the Czech side, caused by Slovak separatist tendencies. By the fall of 1991 I had prolonged the existence of our common state by pushing through the Czecho-Slovak fiscal transfer one more time (despite the very hostile resistance of Pithart's Czech government).

I have repeatedly mentioned the key phrase,

4. I have been comparing the intra-German fiscal transfer with our GDP for a long time. Recently it was brought to my attention that in the past two decades Germany was annually (!) transferring into the former GDR the equivalent of the entire Marshall plan which was designed for fifteen countries, not one, and for a period of three years. Such transfers were done in Germany every year!

fiscal transfer, which seems to be the pivotal word of this time. Should fiscal transfers be done by the EU (despite the fact that the 'treaties', including the Lisbon treaty, say they should not) and should the European integration grouping – silently or loudly – be transformed from monetary union (EMU) into fiscal union (EFU)? Such transformation does not necessarily have to be officially declared: it can be done silently, on the sly, the way it is being done to a large extent already.

The system of fiscal transfers can first be introduced as an exceptional measure. The purchase of state bonds by the European Central Bank can be considered legitimate for problematic, indebted countries. European bonds can be issued, Brussels can start monitoring state budgets of individual countries before these can be approved 'at home'. We can introduce further European taxes, duties and charges as well as mandatory expenditures, which will have to be paid out by individual countries to their citizens. Many more things of this kind can become reality, and I am sorry we are not talking about the future. Most of the things mentioned already exist today, in one form or another, even if they are implemented in a cautious and half-hearted way.

The eurocrats do not see any of this as a problem, which is not surprising, because they have wished to create a European Fiscal Union for a long time.

As a former finance minister and premier, who drafted the state budgets in his time, as a Parliament speaker who approved them (or voted against them), but who signed them and brought them into life in a way similar to my current presidential role, I must say that the state budget (and communal budgets on lower levels) is the axis of governance. It is because of state budgets that governments fall, it is the budget that often triggers a no-confidence vote, it is always the biggest political conflict of the year, defining the main financial flows in the country, affecting the daily lives of millions of people.

Is it possible to give up on our own state budget? I remember well my efforts to explain to the people of the still whole and undivided Czechoslovakia in the first months of 1990 that the state budget was their own budget, that it was not something that existed outside their lives and that they had to look after it through their elected deputies. I have a feeling I was successful then and the people took the state budget seriously for the first time in 50 years. Am I expected to tell them as president that this is no longer true? Shall I tell them it is a purely technocratic issue, which can be handled for us by an Estonian or Spanish Euro-Commissioner who happens to be in charge of these matters in the European government, or more correctly, the European Commission? I will most certainly do no such thing, and for the rest of my presidential days I will not sign such a treaty. My guilt for signing the Lisbon treaty is great enough as it is.

The acceleration of European integration started with the ratification of the Maastricht Treaty in 1991. We accepted it through signing the Treaty of Accession to the EU, which preceded our *de facto* joining the EU on 1 May 2004. This treaty formulated, among other things, the so-called Maastricht convergence criteria (I started my polemic about their relevance many years ago by proposing to accept our

104

own Česká Lípa (Boehmisch Leipa) or Český Brod (Boehmischbrod) criteria[5] which define the conditions of membership for individual countries in the EU).

From the viewpoint of the eurozone – not a country seeking membership – I always considered the Maastricht criteria to be wrong and in fact uninteresting. As an economist and politician I considered the permitted 3 per cent of state budget deficit to be absurdly high. It was not imaginable to me that we could ever allow such a huge deficit. I remember our efforts to avoid a big budget deficit through austerity 'packages' in the spring of 1997, when it was becoming obvious that the economy was slowing down, after our own or rather Mr. Tošovský's central bank 'stepped on the brakes.'[6] The scale

5. 'Klaus' criteria for the adoption (or non-adoption) of a common European currency', Lidové noviny, 20 January 2006. Reprinted in the book *Year Four* (2007), Prague: Euromedia.
6. See my 'Three years after the currency crisis' in the eponymous CEP proceedings, No. 5, 2000, but also Kočárník's argument in his text 'Fifteen years after the currency crisis in the Czech Republic' *Today's world*, (2011) Prague: Fragment, pp. 147–50.

of those austerity measures – when our GDP was nominally much smaller – greatly exceeds the scale of Mr. Kalousek's cuts today.

What does the magic figure of 3 per cent mean? Does it mean it is possible that countries with a long-term balance or even a surplus in their budget and countries with a long-term deficit of 3 per cent can exist side by side? (I leave aside the much higher deficits in Europe and the Czech Republic today, something that is beyond my wildest imagination). There is no question that our high deficits at home were produced by Social Democratic governments headed by Zeman, Špidla, Gross and Paroubek (see arguments in my book *Where Tomorrow Begins*[7]. I am convinced that in the long-term a monetary union cannot exist very well with different deficits ranging from 0 to 3 per cent of GDP. It is possible only in the short-term.

Even the unfortunate Keynes, who opened the door to the present horrifying deficits by defending budget deficits as such (they were rightly considered a social evil before his time)

7   (2009), Prague: Euromedia, part III, Chapter 2.

never meant deficits to be permanent! Even Keynes saw budget deficits as 'medication', usable only in times of low aggregate demand, in other words in crisis. Whether this is the right cure for crises has been subject to debate among economists for decades. I belong to those who think that deficit financing is no cure – after all, it was well illustrated in the Great Depression of the 1930s, the Japanese decade of stagnation in the 1990s and the total failure of attempts to cure the crisis of the last decade through American deficits. Keynes's famous multiplier has a very limited value. Keynes assumed that in times of economic prosperity, the deficit would be paid back from the budget surplus. None of that is true in Europe today.

There is a more complex question: whether the current form of democratic government allows balanced budgets in the long-term, even when counted on aggregate over several years. The first to make this point were Buchanan and Wagner in 1977 in *Democracy in Deficit: The Political Legacy of Lord Keynes*. One of their most important followers, P. J. Boettke, together with S. A. Beaulier, said in that regard that Keynesianism was a 'serious disease', which could be fatal for the functioning of democracy.[8]

However tempting deficit financing may seem in theory, in practice it has not worked, in the Czech Republic or in Europe.

I firmly believe that giving up the state budget means giving up statehood. Do we need any more arguments? I do not think so, but it appears the European Union is headed precisely in the direction of taking control of our national budgets and hence taking control of our nations. And there is no consolidated political power opposing it.

It seems we could opt for a middle game here, a temporary, emergency solution. It is possible to say that a mistake was made by allowing countries with a latent deficit into the eurozone, and that the cost of this acceptance – which was not a fraudulent break-in on the part of those countries, but a consequence

8. In his article 'Deficits, Debts and Debasement', Cato Policy Report, No.4, 2011.

of an invitation to them – will have to be shared by the 'inviting' countries as well. Pay up in one lump sum, settle the debt and start from zero. The countries with chronic deficits will either have to leave the eurozone, or introduce a radical systemic cure (similar to our post-communist transformation), turning themselves into countries without a chronic deficit. What we need is a one-time outright transfer and a resolute, non-hybrid solution for countries receiving the aid. Only that could prevent the emergence of EFU. But for how long?

The question is whether those responsible for the invitation (and approval of membership) are willing to accept this solution, because they, too, have their Buchanan-Wagnerian 'democratic' governments. I naturally think this would be in all respects a cheaper and easier solution for them. But the invitation and membership approval were not put forth by Merkel and Sarkozy but by Chirac and Kohl. Will their successors feel sufficiently responsible for the decisions of their predecessors? Will they convince the current electorate that they are only paying for old mistakes, and that

Sarkozy and Merkel (and others) are essentially innocent? I am afraid this is not how politics works.

I also think that the positives of economic integration in Europe were misunderstood, and the benefits of territorial market expansion have reached their limits. (In fact, economic integration has now led to sub-optimum solutions typical of attempts at regional integration. In particular, we have lost the advantage of trading freely with the rest of the world. Economists know that apart from 'trade creation', regional integration leads also to 'trade diversion'.) The regional market expansion of Europe was quite unnaturally accompanied by excessive control (regulation, forced harmonization and standardization, in fact blocking), which put the market in a straitjacket of a common currency, artificially imposed on this larger and quite heterogeneous area.

The former British finance minister, Nigel Lawson, wrote in *The Times* at the beginning of September 2011: 'The decision to embark on European Monetary Union was among the most irresponsible political initiatives in the post-war world'.[9]

This was not the end of it. Slowing the market down through environmentalist interventions is currently the latest in line of the most dangerous and vicious elements of control and regulation.

European economic integration has already exhausted its potential for improvement of Europe's economic performance having made the transition from closed (or semi-closed) economic models to open economies before World War II, and increasingly during that time. These economies were at least formally open, although all kinds of hidden protectionism still persisted (our business companies could tell many a horrifying tale along those lines). It was more of a single step upwards, as illustrated by Figure 1:

9. 'We Need a Constitution to Protect Us from a Superstate', *The Times*, 5 September 2011.

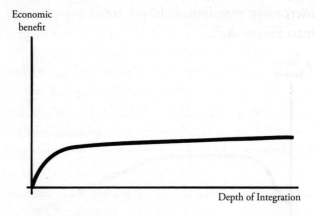

rather than an enduring upward curve, which would be illustrated by Figure 2:

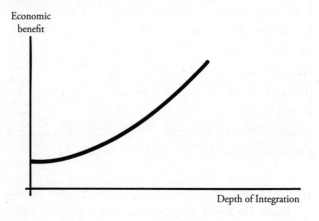

I am afraid the eurocrats think we are in Figure 2. I think we are in Figure 1, which, thanks to increasing regulation, has a tendency to turn into Figure 3:[10]

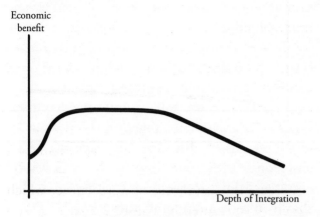

Economic benefit

Depth of Integration

I do not know whether we can change this. It is possible that it will be up to the rest of the world, particularly through increasing competition from the BRIC countries, to bring dynamism to the European economy, and that it will be their pressure that will lead to a gradual change of our attitude. In a cruel paradox for the eurocrats, this could be a solution.

10. Incidentally, Kenneth Minogue in his very valuable book *The Servile Mind* (Encounter Books: London, 2010) uses roughly the same diagram. His vertical coordinate uses the expression 'integrated area's performance' which is the same thing.

113

We could talk about a thousand other things, about the ageing population of Europe, the double-edged consequences of increasing nominal education for a constantly growing number of Europeans (accompanied by poems on the 'education society'), while all forms of productively usable education are shrinking rapidly, we could talk about the counter-productivity of fashionable anti-discriminatory measures, the absurdity of fighting CO_2 emissions, the misleading faith in salvation coming from information technologies, but that would be a different story.

FOUR

The pitfalls of denationalization and communitarization of Europe

The European ideology (europeism, in brief) is based on the idealistic theory of the state, something the eurocrats try to implement on a continental level, having failed to accomplish it on the national level in the past. It is based on the idea that states, more precisely the nation states, represent the Evil – because they were once the cause of wars among other things – while the supranational, continental and global entities represent the Good, because they – according to eurocrats – eliminate all forms of nationalist bickering once and for all. This view is obviously childish, yet it is generally accepted in Europe.

On the one hand this view is part of a broader ideology of 'global governance', which is a truly global trend today. One week at the UN General Assembly in New York in mid-September 2011 is enough to make you see that this is a generally accepted view there, shared by all those who cannot wait to start governing globally. In fact they think – rightly to an extent – that they are already doing so. I have made many public references to this phenomenon over the years. Perhaps a little surprisingly for some, the most resolute pronouncement came in a speech on 28 October 2010, when I said:

It is not possible to ignore the fact that efforts at 'integration' on the part of political elites in the largest countries of the world are increasingly shifting from social-engineering projects designed for individual states and continents to projects with a truly intercontinental or even a global dimension. In that sense, current economic problems in many places around the world provide a catalyst and accelerator for very problematic developments.

We see that a group of the economically most powerful and politically most influential states of the world seek to become the informal precursors to a global government. A government clearly detached from the democratic legitimacy previously given by citizens, a government which, whatever its formal framework, will *de facto* run our lives without any participation or influence on our part.

In this structure, the phenomenon of citizenship will disappear quickly. Democracy without the citizen is an oxymoron and the frivolous concept of world citizenship is nothing but a manipulation, a mystification confusing the issues. History knows countless examples of nations without a state, but there can be no state without a nation. There can be no state without its citizens. There can be no state without its political people, changing or correcting its present and future, through the democratic process – through the elected representatives.

It is to world domination that the prevailing political, economic and media elites aspire: a world without democratic political legitimacy constantly reaffirmed by the citizens. This is where we see the very concrete and practical contours of the new, very different world to come.[1]

In 2011, John Fonte's *Sovereignty or Submission*,[2] an almost canonical explanation of this problem from viewpoints very close to

1. 'The Speech of 28 October 2010 on the meaning of our state', in *Year Eight*, (2011), Prague: Euromedia.
2. John Fonte, (2011), *Sovereignty or Submission: Will Americans Rule Themselves or Be Ruled by Others?*, Encounter Books: New York.

mine, was published in the United States. I was asked to write an endorsement printed on the book's dust jacket. Here it is:

John Fonte accurately identifies the coalition of institutions, interests and individuals that are promoting global governance and convincingly argues against their attempts to undermine the democratic nation-state. Whatever formal structure it might have, a global government would, in effect, control our lives, with no possibility for us to exert any real influence on it. In such a world order, the concept of citizenship would rapidly become extinct. But democracy without citizens is a contradiction in terms, and the currently popular 'world citizenship' is only mystification and manipulation. My experience with one of its variants, the European Union, is not positive at all.

John Fonte says at the beginning of his book:

Major political leaders and intellectuals tell us that today's global issues are too complex for the 'obsolete' nation-state system; that 'global problems require global solutions'; that sovereignty must be redefined as something that is 'shared' or 'pooled'.

I think it is important that Fonte does not dispute the existence of globalization. He understands that resisting globalization is naive and that the question whether we should welcome it or reject it is beside the point. According to Fonte, the only valid question is what form will the future system have: 'Should it be international, i.e. based on sovereign states, or rather transnational and supranational?'

He defines his terms clearly: 'international' denotes relations between sovereign nation states, 'transnational' means intrusions into the domestic affairs of nation states from across or beyond national borders, 'supranational' means transferring decision-making authority from the nation state to 'global' institutions.

Names of individual chapters clearly indicate what his position is:

Global Governance vs. Self-Government
Liberalism under Assault

The Rise of Transnationalism
The European Union: A Model of Global
Governance
The Suicide of Liberal Democracy?

In the preface to his book, John O'Sullivan
(the current vice president of RFE in Prague)
says:

'Global governance' is another political
system or regime. It seeks to take
ultimate political power from parliaments
and congresses accountable to national
electorates in sovereign states, and to vest it
in courts, bureaucracies, NGOs, and various
transnational bodies that are accountable
only to themselves or to other transnational
bodies ... In the academy, the media, the
law, the foreign policy establishment, the
corporate world, the wider political elite
and – almost inevitably – the bureaucracies that serve international institutions
and nongovernmental organizations, the
ideology of global governance is the
prevailing orthodoxy ... 'global governance'
is another political system or regime. It
seeks to take ultimate political power from

parliaments and congresses accountable to national electorates in sovereign states, and to vest it in courts, bureaucracies, NGOs, and various transnational bodies that are accountable only to themselves or to other transnational bodies ...[3]

These sentences are very poignant.[4]

I consider the unification of Europe and the attempts at European governance to be two variants of the same theme, albeit on a smaller scale. The ideas are identical. The ambition to abolish the states, which allegedly cause wars, by weakening them and siphoning their competences upwards to Brussels or downwards to the regions, is supported by a hypothesis (never defined, or rather never seriously defined) of so-called subsidiarity, which has the full magic of hegelian-marxist permanent fluidity and elusiveness (I remember that in my student years at the end of the 1950s I had a feeling

3. O'Sullivan in Fonte, op. cit, pp. ix–x.
4. Jeremy Rabkin offered very similar arguments, a decade earlier, in his book *Why Sovereignty Matters* (1998), Washington: American Enterprise Institute.

of unbelievable retardation because I was unable to understand marxist dialectics, and I remember having tortured my teachers by asking them for a simple explanation).

The dialectic magic of subsidiarity lies in the fact that it works every time, regardless of the amount of centralization or decentralization, regardless of whether we choose to move towards centralization or decentralization. It works regardless of what we are trying to prove. Those of us who have lived under Communism know that democratic centralism was defined with similar 'dialectics'. Its structural similarity with the phenomenon of subsidiarity is awesome.[5]

I keep harassing the eurocrats with a question about how it is possible that the EU (and all its previous forms) have been fully in line with the principles of subsidiarity in 1960, 1970, 1980, 1990, 2000 or 2010 although the allocation

5. John Laughland reminds us in his book *The Tainted Source* (Little, Brown & Company, London; 1st edition, 1997) that subsidiarity is a corporativistic doctrine, originally formulated in the Vatican in the early years of Italian fascism.

124

of competencies changed dramatically over the years, while the citizens – and their inherent ability to decide about matters concerning them – remain the same, living in the same places.

For two decades I have been saying that it is necessary to use economic terminology and look for 'public goods' in territories of different size, in order to find out what are the public goods on the level of a community, city, region (province or Bundesland), state, and perhaps even a group of states or an entire continent. I cannot imagine well-defined public goods on the level of the whole planet.

I am also convinced there is one undisputable regularity – the further from the individual citizen we go, the less real the public goods are. The fact that the EU decides on many more matters than the individual states today, is in no contradiction to this regularity. It only means that some public goods, naturally belonging to lower levels of decision, were transferred to the headquarters in Brussels.

We can seriously argue about where exactly the public goods belong, but one thing is certain: democracy can function no higher than the level of the state. This is a thesis I keep presenting around the world – in Czech, German, English, Italian – and the response to it is zero, nothing. I have never heard a single argument about how democracy could function on a higher level, such as a group of states or a union.

The argument that democracy requires its demos, or people, is banal by now, and nobody is doubting it, probably because in reality, eurocrats do not care about democracy one bit. Nigel Lawson again: 'A fundamental contempt for democracy has always been one of the most striking and least attractive characteristics of the European movement'.[6]

Similarly David Goodhart: 'The 'European Idea rests somewhat more openly upon hostility to European nations and their national identities'.[7]

At the beginning of September 2011, I spoke

6. Lawson, op. cit.
7. Goodhart, David, *The Guardian*, 24 February 2004.

about these things at a conference in Cernobbio near Lago di Como about the democratic deficit of the EU and about post-democracy, and Mario Monti[8], former European commissioner and rector of the Milan University, replied with these words: 'In a group of 27 countries the decisions must be asymmetric'.

What is an asymmetric decision? It must be that somebody has the right to make decisions and somebody else does not! I cannot come up with any other intepretation. Nobody in the audience protested. I guess it was no accident. Quite logically, eurocrats love post-democracy. They can make their decisons behind the backs of the citizens, which is why they love everything that comes from Brussels.

The voters are a 'scattered' group of people even in the nation state (while the pressure groups can be, and therefore are, well organized), but on the level of Europe, the voters are even more

8. I can but smile when I read the book *Darkness at Noon* by Arthur Koestler, the well-known author, thinker and opponent of Communism who once said that the expression 'European Commissioner', was a good terminological choice by the EU.

'scattered' or lost than in the nation state. The famous American thinker Francis Fukuyama makes the point precisely in saying that inevitably there is 'the vacuum of international legitimacy above the level of the nation state'.[9] And life in that vacuum is what eurocrats want.

I can support my opinions with quotes from a number of other authors both Czech and international, but it is the text of Professor Fiala that touches my imagination when he says that Europe recently became home to a 'very dangerous idea that the nation state must be eliminated'. He says:

> The European elite, consisting of politicians, businessmen and intellectuals ... has managed to penetrate the minds of European citizens with the idea that preservation of peace, securing of prosperity and general satisfaction is only possible when the nation state is overcome.[10]

9. Fukuyama, Francis (2002), 'Has History Restarted Since 11 September?' *CIS*, Sydney, Occasional Paper No. 81.
10. Fiala, op. cit., p. 6.

I do not know how easy that penetration was, but the fact is that the citizens – and I do not accept the expression 'European citizens', I use, out of principle, the expression 'citizens of European states', because I do not consider myself to be a European citizen, I consider myself to be an inhabitant of Europe – have not protested very much in the course of the last decades.

There are many reasons for the lack of protest among the citizens, one of them being that they never really decided on this matter and therefore do not know much about it (it would be interesting and honest to ask them that question one day). Also, nobody explained it to them. They do not know that states are already in the process of *de facto* liquidation.

In the words of Owen Harries, the citizens do not know that:

> … in a sense nation states are being attacked from above and below: above by pseudo, quasi, international or universal organisations – we have international courts, we have inter- national this and that – but also from below,

with all these forces coming up to challenge the power of the nation-state – everything from environmentalists to drug gangs ...[11]

People are angry about various interventions from Brussels, but they do not think about what makes them possible. Professor Fiala says quite rightly that:

The importance of the nation state lies not in the fact that it is national (many of them do not even fall into this category) but the fact that it creates a comprehensible space, a source of identity and civic loyalty. And thanks to that democracy can be exercised.[12]

As I said earlier, there is no other place where democracy can function. I do not know what else I should add to this.

The following thesis is equally important: 'The non-existence of supranational European

11. Harries, Owen (Autumn 2002), Policy Magazine, Centre for Independent Studies, Sydney.
12. Fiala, op. cit.

democracy weakens the functioning democracies of European nation states'.

Yes, thanks to the EU, our democracy is worse,
not better – contrary to what we are being
told. And we are not alone in this. I gave
warnings a long time ago that joining the EU
will not strengthen democracy, it will weaken
it. These warnings were labeled eurosceptic,
even anti-european. Yet it was just an empirical
judgement, a consequence of looking around
with some attention.

In Jiří Weigl's very poignant speech in Berlin in
May 2010, identity is considered to be 'society's
essential cement, assuring its cohesion, creating
the feeling of togetherness which in turn brings
about social solidarity'.[13]

When he speaks about so-called shared European
values, such as Christianity, humanism, Jewish-
Greek roots, and the Enlightenment in the
fading democratic tradition, he says:

13. 'Europe and National Identity from the Czech
    Perspective', CEP Newsletter, August 2010, p. 1.

These values are undoubtedly present in the societies of individual EU member states with different intensities and to a different extent, but their citizens very seldom see them as values shared by all.[14]

He also presents an important thesis that:

The unifying power (of these shared values), is far from being able to compensate whatever divides the European nations. (…) The perception of European togetherness and European identity is derivative, secondary and in many cases only emerging. Some people do not want to take this into consideration.[15]

Likewise, Petr Hájek says:

While the political elites, almost in unison, work with great intensity on the construction of the European state, the position of the public in most countries is one of indifference, bordering on mistrust: they are

14. Ibid.
15. Ibid.

far from sharing their governments' enthusiasm for integration.[16]

I have been saving for a long time Professor Emanuele Ottolenghi's paper 'Can Europe Do Away with Nationalism'[17] which calls any potential European identity a 'distant dream'. He emphasizes the importance of 'social cohesion' and does not believe that society, 'divided by different identities, values and historical narratives', can be united by 'abstract rights and duties under EU treaties and regulations'. For him, citizenship is not an abstract idea of rights and obligations, we do not choose citizenship, we are born into it, citizenship grows out of our shared history, shared experience, and often also shared suffering.

I am convinced, that the abstract European idea can never be a sufficient substitution for national identity. That is why 'public apathy' is to be expected. During emotional moments

16. Hájek, Petr (2009), *Smrt ve Středu*, Prague: Dokořán, p. 210.
17. American Enterprise Institute, European Outlook, May–June 2005.

of Bush's (or rather Rumsfeld's) conflict with Europe – as much as it may be a little passé right now – we hear the argument that 'anti-americanism and the fantastic concept of Europe's status as a superpower' are the wrong basis for europeanism.

Roger Scruton also has interesting things to say in his book *The Need for Nations*, but I will quote him from an excerpt published under the same title in the Czech magazine Kontexty. I was pleased to notice that he writes about the 'EU's adoption of the ecclesiastical doctrine of 'subsidiarity', in order to remove powers from member states under the pretence of granting them'.[18]

I do not consider subsidiarity to be dogmatic in itself: it is its authoritarian and involuntary enforcement that I mind. However, its charmingly elusive, arbitrarily definable emptiness is described by Scruton with great precision.

18. Scruton, Roger (2006), *The Need for Nations*, London: Civitas: Institute for the Study of Civil Society, quoted here from an excerpt published under the same title in the Czech magazine, Kontexty, No. 4, 2011, p. 16.

He sees the evolution of integration in the same way – the elites will eventually and inevitably push through 'transnational government, under a common system of law, in which national loyalty will be no more significant than support for a local football team ...'[19]

Professor Scruton is convinced that 'the nation state has proven its worth as a stable basis for democratic governments' and that is why we should improve it, not reject it'. It is painful for me, too, whenever the nation state is identified with nationalism. That is why I have to agree with Scruton that 'nationalism is part of the pathology of national loyalty, not its natural condition'.

Roger Scruton furthermore mentions Chesterton, who once said:

> ... to condemn patriotism because people go to war for patriotic reasons, is like condemning love because some loves lead to murder ...

19. Ibid., p. 17.

Scruton, as an Englishman, must insist that:

> ... nazism would never have been defeated had it not been for the national loyalty of the British people who were determined to defend their homeland against invasion.[20]

And I will offer one more quote from him:

> ... Those who believe that the division of Europe into nations has been the primary cause of European wars should remember the devastating wars of religion that national loyalties finally brought to an end ...[21]

This kind of thinking is close to mine. In my speech on 28 October 2010, I said:

> We are not a statistical sum of individual, lonely human beings, we are a community of more than ten million citizens, members of one broad family where people understand

20. Ibid., p. 24.
21. Ibid., p. 24.

one another not only because they use the same language, but also because of their traditions, historical experience, specific culture and, in the most general terms possible, their common interests ...

Does the state, that we have taken over from our ancestors as a specific and unique heritage, have any meaning and purpose in the present world? Do we really feel it as something that is deep in our minds and hearts? Do we not accept it only as some neutral, easily replaceable entity? Is it not becoming a mere 'administrative unit' for which we no longer have any deep, personal feelings?

If that is so, ... we should admit to ourselves that we are the generation that is knowingly giving up on the Czech state; that the thousand year-long tradition has come to an end; that the rightful place for our inherited traditions, habits, culture and way of thinking is now in a skansen of folklore curiosities, because life, to use the words of one of our important sceptical writers, is elsewhere.

137

If that is not so, as for most of us it is not, if we still share the authentic perception of our common national existence as something different from the national existence of the Germans, Russians, Americans, French, British and other fully fledged nations, we have to realize what the consequences are. In that case, we vitally need our anchor, our state and we are right to call to mind the hard-won heritage, traditions and experience of our ancestors. In that case, we must defend the existence and values of this state.

At any rate, it is clear that national as well as territorial loyalties are the precondition for democratic governance. It seems equally obvious that the European continent is not a space suitable for territorial or national loyalty. You cannot grasp this diversity in one *Augenblick* – from Cyprus to Finland, from Portugal to Estonia. Therefore, no nation called European exists, and no such nation ever did exist. That is why the entire concept of the 'ever-closer Europe' of unification, central-ization, harmonization and standardization (you could call it *Gleichschaltung*) and utmost suppression of the nation state, is a wrong concept.

Eurocrats seem to know this, and that is why they do not talk about the national or continental principle. Instead, they talk about the 'communitarian' principle, which is yet another undefined and undefinable legal cliche, which can cover – and conceal at the same time – whatever it desires. The great and much too self-confident lawyers of the 'European law' naturally cannot defend this principle in any way: they just use it as something that descended from above, without any arguments supporting it – whether things are right or wrong, functional or dysfunctional, positive or negative, all they have to do is just say it is 'communitarian' or compliant with the communitarian law.

Tomáš Břicháček is a rarity – a lawyer with a critical mind. He said in his speech at the CEP seminar: '[t]he trend towards centralization is part of the genetic equipment of the EU' because the legal framework of the

EU is based on the 'risky communitarian concept'.[22]

He also says that 'the concept of subsidiarity is so flexible it can be interpreted in all kinds of ways' because it is based on 'very vague criteria, that anybody can fill with whatever they wish'.[23]

Like Fiala and Scruton, he says that unlike the nation state 'the Union does not represent a comprehensible, transparent, internally cohesive public space'.[24]

He sees the genetic defect of the EU in the competencies inevitably shifting towards the centre, because:

- the EU legislative process is fully in the hands of the Union's institutions;
- 'the interest of the Union's institutions

22. Published in *European Union in the Trap of Centralization: CEP Proceedings*, No. 90, (2011) pp. 11 and 12.
23. Ibid., p. 15.
24. Ibid., p. 18.

runs contrary to the slowing down of the EU expansion and their own powers.'[25]

Lukáš Petřík, who also took part in the seminar, shared the opinion that representative democracy can only function on the level of a nation state. He asks the clever question:

Do the people of European states watch the same pan-European TV news? Do they read the same pan-European paper? Is there a common European language, a history interpreted in a common way, common traditions, common values, solidarity and interest?[26]

With equal rationality, he gives a list of European commissioners and asks whether anybody knows these names. He adds:

We know our politicians. We know who is Klaus, Kalousek, Nečas, Sobotka, Hašek, Bárta, Grebeníček. And we can fire them in

25. Ibid., p. 15.
26. Ibid., p. 22.

the elections. We cannot do the same with European Commissioners.[27]

Alexandr Tomský, speaking at the same seminar, feels the 'spirit of jacobinism', when European elites try to create:

a new, centralized Europe and a new man without traditions, without nations, without a Church, an atomized, powerless society of total equality and moral as well as intellectual relativism, which is the very essence of utopia.[28]

My favorite American commentator, George Will, notices that:

the European Union has a flag no one salutes, an anthem no one sings, a president no one can name, a parliament (in Strasbourg) no one other than its members wants to have power (which must subtract from the powers of national legislatures), a capital (Brussels) of coagulated bureaucracy

27. Ibid., p. 23.
28. Ibid., p. 32.

no one admires or controls, a currency that presupposes what neither does nor should nor soon will exist.

I am saying all this because I want to emphasize the fact that this more or less absurd European situation is being noticed by an increasing number of people (and I could quote many more, these were just texts I had at my bedside while recovering from flu). Unfortunately politicians as well as citizens are not moved by them. Can there be stronger, wittier, more revealing or convincing arguments? I do not know.

There are no arguments in favour of destroying the nations of Europe and replacing them with a unified superstate on the basis of 'communitarism'. If there were any such arguments, they would be arguments in favour of the destruction of democracy, and of control over the continent by an unelected elite. And those arguments would not be too different from the arguments of those who tried to control Europe in the past.

A brief digression into the world of Czech politics

Czech politicians and their view of these matters deserve our attention, too. At first glance we should expect to see the right wing being *a priori* sceptical, or at least increasingly sceptical over time, of the utopian social-engineering project for a new and better Europe. The Right should realize with increasing clarity that Maastricht and even more the Lisbon shift represent an increasing threat to the sovereignty of the Czech Republic, while reducing the democratic legitimacy of European structures. The Right should appreciate that these treaties entail more centralism and dirigism and fewer real civic freedoms, while we are lured towards gradual substitution of those values by 'human rights' that are only formalized because they are unenforceable.

Conversely, one would expect the Left, which, unlike the Right, is much better organized in Europe – to push more and more towards accelerated federalization, i.e. the final victory of the European non-liberal project. The

Socialist International has had the European integration process firmly under its thumb from the start, regardless of election results in individual countries.

In reality we see quite a different picture. Those parliamentary political parties that define themselves 'at home' as right-wing (or, in the modern Newspeak, 'centre-right') nearly unanimously support the supranational project. History shows clearly that this is true for the Civic Democratic Alliance, the Christian Democrats, the People's Party or Freedom Union and recently TOP 09, to name a few. Some new parties standing outside Parliament, parties that appeared on our scene only after the country joined the EU – such as the party of Jana Bobošíková, Vladimír Železný or Petr Mach – are 'euro-realistic', although their politics (with the exception of the Freedom Party) do not have strong right-wing views. Their political platform is defined by fears for the Czech national interest rather than by ideological reservations about the integration project itself, and their influence in the Czech Republic is limited.

We see the same paradox on the Left. The Communist Party – representing a stable 15 per cent share of the electorate – is somewhat opposed to the EU, because it sees the direction of the European project as not leftist enough. The Czech Social Democrats see their support for 'hard-core' European integration as a legitimate part of their political job, regardless of whether this is in the interest of the Czech Republic or not. In that respect they are, thanks to the Socialist International, already a 'European' and not a Czech political party. (The same is true for our People's Party and its links with the European People's Party in the European Parliament).

There are other non-parliamentary political parties on the left, such as the Greens, whose internationalist character is nothing but an informal 'International'. As the federal EU is constructed, these groupings play the role of the proverbial 'fifth column' in the Czech Republic. Many lobbies, including political, corporativist and business groups, share these positions, because their narrow interests fare better in an environment with a deep democratic deficit. Naturally, we should not forget the informal political group called 'the Media' through which europeists exert their pressure on politicans as well as the general public.

The Civic Democratic Party is a specific example. When I was chairman of this party and even shortly after I stepped down, it was the only relevant political force on the Czech scene – and in fact on the entire European continent – that based its critique of the overwhelming integration on actual ideas. It knew the difference between the time before Maastricht and after. It kept explaining to the Czech people, enchanted as they were by the slogan of 'returning to Europe' in the first decade after the collapse of Communism, that the country has always been and always will be a part of Europe, that that is why we have to look after our interests ourselves, because nobody else is going to do it for us. And that, despite much noble and emotional rhetorics, the EU is not primarily an altruistic project designed to 'uplift and fraternize' the nations of Europe. The Civic Democratic Party never ceased to explain that the European project is primarily a power gambit played by Germany and France in a distinctly socialist style, with a number of elements similar to those that we were so happy to get rid of after 1989. It explained that we cannot stay outside the integration project, but that it is our duty to take part in it while maintaining our national sovereignty and taking a rational approach. The Civic Democratic Party made it clear that the main thing we can contribute in the defense of our interests is our historic experience with the utopian social-engineering projects of centrally directed empires, two variants of which we have involuntarily experienced.

This was a natural position for the Civic Democrats at first. By the logic of things, as party chairman and premier, I applied for EU membership and the party said Yes in the accession referendum in 2004. The flip-side of the same coin was our fundamental reservation about the direction in which the European project was headed, particularly after the adoption of the Maastricht Treaty and especially Lisbon. At first, we were shouted down at home and in Europe on the grounds that it was none of our business as long as we were still outside 'the club'. After we became fully-fledged members, the shouting down changed into arguments that we should have made up our minds before joining, and that now we should 'use the good opportunity to shut up', to use the rather straightforward words of Jacques Chirac, the French President.

It is sad to see that there are two Czech positions: one for the people at home and one for the European bureaucracy, the European government and the European Parliament. From the many years of my own experience, I know that most of our ministers, including prime ministers, but also deputies on all levels of the hierarchy, have two faces. They show one to their voters, and the other when speaking in Brussels, at various EU summits and similar events. They talk tough at home, but when they cross the border their resolve to fight for Czech interests fades quickly.

In all fairness, this phenomenon is not limited only to those whom we elect. The two other states, labeled as 'eurosceptic' by the media – Great Britain and Poland – behave similarly. We can see it best with the British Conservatives after Margaret Thatcher. With the full weight of public opinion behind them, sharply opposing the euro and any further transfer of powers to Brussels – winning many a vote thanks to this – as soon as they step onto the Continent, their resolve to fight for these principles evaporates. Poland uses its position to raise its status and become a leader in Central Europe, maximizing its influence as a European 'power'. Such positioning is thoroughly legitimate, but has little to do with ideas, and still less to do with critical views of the European integration process. However, both of these examples characterize the two-fold Czech position very well, too.

Our view of European integration does not, therefore, reflect the left–right division in politics. We can say that from this point of view it is actually the other way around. While leftist voters are on the sceptical side, support for the European project is increasing among the right-wing electorate.

This seemingly paradoxical phenomenon has a relatively easy and logical explanation. Centre-right voters follow the media more carefully and are therefore much more under their influence and pressure, which is overwhelmingly europeistic, with a few minor exceptions. It is debatable to what extent this is caused by the fact that mainstream media in the Czech Republic are in the hands of foreign owners, or whether the reason is their umbilical connection with the superficially attractive intellectual snobbery of 'non-political politics', which is just another synonym for the intellectuals linked in one way or another with the former Czech president, Václav Havel. On the other hand, citizens with leftist tendencies based on their natural social interests do not have such need to bring their views into conformity with the opinions asserted by the news media. Instead, they tend to rely much more on common sense.

During the Czech EU presidency in 2009, a number of Civic Democrats, who have been previously even more critical of the EU than me, became 'diligent Europeans'. This has to do with the effect I have already mentioned. Many of our politicians have 'clear' theoretical understanding of the issues, but day-to-day life in the EU devours them and transforms them. All of a sudden they are on a first-name basis with presidents and premiers of other countries, they take part in various meetings and summits, they give in to the illusion of entering the world of grand politics on a big stage and they are hopelessly dazzled by the limelight.

This is how simple it very often is on a human level. In an environment soaked with 'european faith' it is not easy for our nation's represent-atives in Europe to remember that their duty is to represent the interests of the Czech Republic and its people. They too easily forget that loyalty to the EU should be preceded by loyalty to their own state. 'Euro-deputies' undergo the same transformation. Sooner or later they become one of the 'Brussels people', the tens of thousands of clerks and politicians who are the only real 'demos', the only people of this European federalist project. It is this personal psychology, influenced by tangible interests, that eventually persuades our political representatives to feel more loyalty to the environment they were sent into, rather than to the people who sent them there.

We can reach one general conclusion. For the reasons mentioned above, Czech politicians, regardless of their political orientation do not defend our interests in the EU as they should. We see more or less the same pattern as in local politics. Positions based on principles and ideas – if there were any at all – give in to gradual atrophy, for the benefit of immediate self-advantage. In this way – with exceptions that prove the rule – they jump on the bandwagon of the 'big players' and fall hostage to their interests. I am afraid that in this respect there is no change in sight.

FIVE

Where do we go from here?

I have tried to argue throughout this text that the current European problem is not limited to the Eurozone debt crisis only. The bankruptcy of many European nations is the logical, most visible and most urgent aspect of a more general and more deep-seated problem. The problem is not confined to a crisis in the design of the EU: there are many indications that the entire civilization of the West is in a political, economic and social crisis. The situation in Obama's United States is not qualitatively better. When Rector Fiala of Masaryk's university speaks of the 'weakening of the Occident' in his above-mentioned article, he probably means the same thing.

It is important to realize, accept and think through all the consequences of the fact that other parts of the world are not in a crisis such as ours. There is a certain unwanted irony here. Since their foundation, the Bretton Woods institutions – the International Monetary Fund and the World Bank – have been assisting countries from the developing world only. (After we started our radical economic transformation in the 1990s, they became irrelevant for us, too). Today, these institutions are paradoxically helping mainly the countries of Europe.

The debt crisis, the gradual loss of competitiveness, the permanent decline in economic growth, the crisis of the welfare state, the increasing regulation of all walks of life, the festering social conflicts, the problems of immigration, the political landscape devoid of ideas, the omnipresent manipulation of the media and many other issues, all of these indicate that the word 'crisis' is the right one to use. It is no exaggeration. It is also obvious that this crisis will not be solved by a mere parameter-shift of the socio-economic system, nor perhaps by the more or less resolute actions of a single finance minister. The current European crisis is caused by a wide network of problems. Its solution must be equally wide.

The negative developments and problems are getting worse, and the cost of their solution will grow accordingly. Paying off current debts – however resolute and successful – makes it clear that at least the entire next decade will be a decade of difficulties, cuts and austerity measures, something like the Japanese 'lost decade'. It would be an illusion to think that there is a simple and painless way out of this unpleasant situation. It was possible to anticipate this and as far back as 1998 Milton Friedman said the euro would not survive its first severe crisis. It may survive eventually, but only at enormous cost.

In the most general terms we can say that the urgent and necessary change in Europe may come either as a 'prepared political change' or as a spontaneous, chaotic event with some element of conflict. The costs of the latter solution would undoubtedly be much higher than those of the former.

Immediately after the fall of Communism we also had a choice of two alternatives – either to make an at least partly organized, thought-out, rationally conceived transformation of the system, or wait for spontaneous, uncontrolled developments to take place. There were economists – such as the famous Polish economist Jan Winiecki – who claimed the state and its bureaucratic bodies could not accomplish anything in that respect. They insisted that systemic transformation could not be carried

159

out by the state. Other famous and very vocal foreign advisors and investors in our country (as well as the successful and excessively critical businessmen of today), wanted uncontrolled transformation for totally different reasons – it would make them a lot of money. My objection was always that the transformation must be based on a rational comparison of costs and benefits. I think I was vindicated by reality. Our transformation was completed not only with costs lower than the anarchic version, but also with costs lower than in comparable countries.[1]

The way out of the present European crisis, or the solution for Europe (I wish to differentiate Europe from the European Union), is possible only through the renewal of economic and civic freedoms, alleviation of the unbearable burden of the welfare state and other equally unbearable environmental burdens imposed on the economy (reaching its worst so far in the struggle against CO_2 emissions), through

1. There is more on these and other international comparisons in Klaus and Tomšík (2007), *Macroeconomic Facts of Czech Transformation*, Brno: NC Publishing.

increased competititiveness and flexibility in all walks of life and business, through economic liberalization, deregulation and desubsidization. Some will say this is my 'old' program, but I am convinced that once again this program is right for the here and now. Unfortunately, in the last decade we have gone backwards by suppressing the free market. Among other things we slid backward because the danger of Communism was forgottten – by us, but even more so in Western Europe.

The European Union (I am not talking about Europe now) as an institution can survive, only if it says goodbye to the social-engineering (and therefore utopian) visions of artifical unification of the Continent, and returns to the original concept of cooperation between sovereign member countries, which must be the cornerstone of integration, not its victim.

Let us not look for inspiration in other worlds, let us look for it in our own experience. Whenever Europe was free, without the strait-jacket of social-engineering projects, there was prosperity. Recent history makes us all remember (lately I am tempted to add a question mark to

161

'all') that those parts of Europe that succumbed to one such social-engineering vision – central control and planning, accompanied by limited freedoms for the people – was inefficient, while the part of Europe that was more free was also incomparably better off.

Precisely when the EU started changing into a centrally controlled project, and a social-engineering arena, the project stopped in its tracks. There is nothing else to it. Attempts to impose unified control, unified vision and unified government for the whole world (or for the whole of Europe) will inevitably go bankrupt, and the center of prosperity will move elsewhere. It is already happening.

The European Union – as illustrated earlier by the quote from Jose Barroso's speech to the European Parliament in 2011, a speech that was everything but marginal or irrelevant – intends to cure its dysfunctional project by even larger doses of the same medication – more centralism. From our experience of enforced centralism in the Czech Republic, we see this as a totally absurd idea.

Do we have the energy to change all this? Or rather, do we have the energy to change it through a better alternative political project before it changes spontaneously all by itself? I am not sure. It may be too late. It may be that the other side, which does not mind the chaos, has already prevailed. And which other side is it exactly? Some think that Communism is still lurking somewhere in the shadows, others see Osama bin Ladin and Islamic fundamentalism. The politicizing priest Tomáš Halík, together with too many politically-correct politicians from all parties see evil in the conservatism of Mr. Bátora, others still fear The Prague Castle and its alleged nationalism (and who knows what else). The real danger, which these people do not appreciate (because they are not sensitive to it), is somewhere else altogether.

The essence of the problem is that all of these people have accepted the very controversial thesis formulated by Fukuyama at the beginning of the 1990s (which he himself gradually corrected later), claiming that the liberal-democratic regime based on the existence of the nation state had finally prevailed – first over Fascism (in 1945) then over Communism (in 1990), that we shall also 'beat' the islamists, that there are no further dangers, that the proverbial 'end of history' is finally here, and that the principles of liberalism, of individual rights and of traditional representative democracy have defeated all their competitors.

Today, it does not look as though the West has won. John Fonte is right, in his book quoted earlier, when he says:

> Fukuyama was wrong, because in the meantime the rival ideology, which I call 'transnational progressivism' has become a very strong competitor to liberal democracy and thus a threat for the liberal-democratic nation state[2].

Throughout this book I have been saying that the most typical examples of this transnational progressivism – global governance and the European Union – are overwhelming the liberal democracies and nation states, pushing us into the phase of post-democracy.

2.   Fonte, op. cit., p. 64.

The people's elected representatives in the Czech Republic should regard it as their first duty to protect the existence and sovereignty of the Czech state. They should not give in to pressures from the outside. They should advance our interests. They should not succumb to illusions that somebody else will take care of us better than ourselves.

I think ordinary people in our country understand this better than most of our politicians, activist intellectuals and journalists. This is proven by public opinion polls on the situation inside the EU, by the adoption of the failed euro, by the false multiculturalism, by the hollow political correctness, and by the dissatisfaction of the general public with the omnipresent manipulation by the media. It has become fashionable to say that people like me are alone and isolated in our opinions. That is not true. It is Brussels that is isolated, inward-looking, unlistening, unresponsive. The great British historian Arnold Toynbee in his key work *A Study of History*, says that a civilization starts to commit suicide whenever the leaders stop responding to challenges in an innovative way. We should learn from this.

The present Czech political scene, devoid of ideas, characterized by emotional conflicts over various artificial issues and permanent scandals cultivated by the media, indicates that our politicians do not feel they are up to the fundamental political task of today, and that they are making no preparations to change it. We see repeatedly that our electoral system is producing weak governments, that these governments are victim to what seems to be a permanent electoral race, that there is no political leadership, no loyalty, no responsibility, no ability to reach agreement or compromise. One specific issue is the incredible power of the judiciary, the judges, the so-called 'judicracy'. It is interesting to see that even John Fonte, in the part of his book devoted to the European Union, distinguishes between why the EU is headed towards transnationalism (his answer is that this is an ideological design, but I should add that there are concrete interests at stake, too) and how the EU is going there, showing clearly that it is predominantly the European Court of Justice (and the judges) who are pushing for the extreme unification of the continent in their decisions.

I am afraid that our elected representatives have no ambition to stop these unifying and globalizing processes. Perhaps they are not even fully aware of them. Perhaps they do not understand well enough the post-democratic nature of these processes and the underlying loss of freedom. Loss of freedom does not feel so bad when you are sitting on an airplane commuting between Prague and Brussels or elsewhere on a non-stop tour of European summits.

Still, freedom is the key word. Max Hocutt makes my point precisely:

Freedom is not good only because of its inner substance. Freedom is extremely valuable because it works.[3]

Without freedom we shall never repair Europe. And we should repair it, as soon as possible. Let us take the road towards the OES.

3. Hocutt, Max, (2003) 'Compassion without Charity, Freedom without Liberty: The Political Fantasies of Jean-Jacques Rousseau', *Independent Review*, No. 2, p. 173.

(Organization of European States), rather than the road towards the UEPDR. (Union of European Post-Democratic Republics).

THE END

Index

A page reference in italics indicates a figure; an 'n.' indicates a footnote.